The David Solution

How to reclaim power and liberate your organization

Valerie Stewart

Gower

First published 1990 by Gower Publishing Company Limited, Aldershot, Hampshire.

This paperback edition published 1993
Gower Publishing Company
Gower House
Croft Road
Aldershot
Hampshire GU11 3HR
England

Gower
Old Post Road
Brookfield
Vermont 05036
USA

British Library Cataloguing in Publication Data
Stewart, Valerie
    David Solution: How to Reclaim Power and Liberate Your Organization. – New ed
    I. Title
    658

    ISBN 0 566 02843 3 Hardback
        0 566 07420 6 Paperback

Printed in Great Britain at the University Press, Cambridge

THE DAVID SOLUTION

For Enid Davies

Heiliger Dankgesang

Contents

Preface

It's an odd title for a management book, isn't it? Here's how it came about.

One evening, slumped in front of the television after a hard day's work, accompanied by a bottle of something friendly and the cat, I half opened an eye to notice that they were showing a film on road safety. Traffic was going round Spaghetti Junction at high speed and in high volume. In that drowsy state where the intuition works overtime, it occurred to me that I was watching a great many ordinary people doing extremely complicated tasks; and that they *were* doing these tasks, without coming off or killing themselves, was evident. That set me thinking further about how many other complicated tasks and tough decisions people handle in their everyday lives – their house purchases, bringing up their kids, coping with their taxes and social security, managing a home – and how by and large they do them without too much grief and inefficiency. Which led to the stunning thought:

> Why, in that case, do we assume that once people are employed by an organization, we need to train, cajole, discipline, and motivate them to take the kinds of decisions they can, on the evidence, take perfectly well for themselves? Why, for example, do we send them on time management courses to learn that it's a good idea to write down a list of what you're going to do and tick it all off as it's done? Why do we spend a fortune telling them that people are more likely to do what you want if you listen to them and smile? Why do we load

them with managers' manuals, policy manuals, formal procedures, to tell them what decisions to take? *What is so powerful about the doors of the organization that once behind them, people connive at being disempowered?*

In other words, wouldn't it be much simpler, and much more rewarding, if people felt OK about behaving as skilfully, decisively, and independently at work as they do at home, at leisure, in their hobbies? And I thought of everyone I'd met in my career as a consultant, and how many of them, especially those working in big organizations, had somehow picked up the message that everything which wasn't expressly allowed was forbidden; that you shouldn't go outside what the rule book told you; that risk and initiative were frowned upon. I remembered train journeys where I talked to guards who skilfully fostered problem children, or bred champion sheepdogs, but weren't allowed to spend a fiver of the company's money on a taxi for a disrupted customer; car assembly workers who wouldn't tolerate the slightest defect in the model aeroplanes they made, but had long since ceased to care about the poor quality of the product they were paid for; managers who wouldn't do anything to rock the boat at work, but got up at six on a Saturday morning to perfect a new golf stroke. I don't suppose that anybody likes doing less than their best, or turning away customers unsatisfied, so how does it come about that so many people are condemned to spend at least eight hours a day underperforming?

I spend more than half my time working in organizations whose climates are bureaucratic, low-risk systems, rather than customer-focused; where managers are reluctant to take decisions; where innovation is frowned on and failures noticed far more than successes; where there are shelves of reports and analyses that have never been acted on; where people at all levels have an attitude of 'I didn't do it because nobody told me I could'. The saddest thing is that those organizations often spend fortunes on artificial systems and procedures intended to replace the initiative, caring, and entrepreneurial flair that the climate has suppressed: quality circles or briefing groups, introduced without top management commitment to listening to the results; ra-ra conferences on customer care, whose effect will wear off in three months; expensive training courses teaching skills which will never be used because the environment prohibits it; and so on. How much simpler if we could tackle the problem at its root, and stop the organization disempowering people!

Then I remembered what Michelangelo was reported to have said when they asked him how he made his statue of David:

It's easy. You just chip away the bits that don't look like David.

And that's what this book is about. It's for anybody who works in organizations and is depressed or angry at disempowerment – their own or other people's. It's about how to reclaim the David in all of us, however encrusted he may have been by bureaucracy, ignorance, bad management, or the sheer inability to believe that it's OK to come to work with your leading edge glowing. It's about turning around organizations, because people make up organizations.

It's a short book, because the answers are fairly simple; it's putting them into practice that takes the time. It doesn't contain much theory (though a splendid chap called Kurt Lewin once said that there is nothing so practical as a good theory). And it's written from my own personal experiences of chipping away with the chisel, looking for the David, because I hate waste, and wasted human potential is the worst waste of all.

So, if you read the words above and they spoke to you – read on. I've tried to describe the different layers beneath which David lies: the bureaucracy, paralysis by analysis, adherence to the rule book, and other constraints. More importantly, I've tried to suggest ways in which you can reclaim your own David, help other people find theirs, and transform your organization.

1   Chipping away the marble

When Michelangelo looked at the block of marble he was to carve, he looked beyond the outside and saw the shape of the statue he was to create. He could see the real beauty hidden within the waste. The first stage in achieving your own David – the real you, the empowered manager working in an empowering organization – is to do some similar visualization.

The word *visualization* is important. Often we are too driven by words and figures in our thinking, and we don't realize the contribution that our other senses and feelings could and should contribute when we're planning what kind of people we want to be and what sort of organization we want to be part of. I'm certain that Michelangelo didn't begin by working out David's height and weight and size in socks; he would have thought in terms of feelings, impressions, the kind of impact he wanted the finished statue to make. And the first step in reclaiming freedom – for yourself or your organization – is a process of visualization, where you detach yourself from the balance sheets and the performance indicators and the Management by Objectives system, and ask instead: 'What do I want this place, what do I want me, to *feel* like when we've made things better?'

The best way to do this is as a team exercise. Even better, when several teams from the same organization do it and share their results. You need lots of paper, magic markers, flat surfaces, etc., and then you ask the team or teams to draw a picture which represents the ideal organization, as they see it. The only rule is that they don't come up with the standard organization chart, or use lots of words and figures: they have to produce an image, a metaphor, and then be prepared to say what the metaphors stand for.

When you try this, there'll be stunned silence for a while; great big grown-ups aren't used to drawing kiddies' pictures. Then what happens is that people start to talk about what they want their drawing to represent: in other words, they talk about their values and feelings, and how they will represent them on paper. It takes a good couple of hours, and it works.

If you've managed to do this with more than one team, you can then have each team talk through their drawings to one another. Often, you'll find the same concept represented in different ways. In Telecom New Zealand, one group drew an athlete passing the finishing line, with various bits of background indicating the glare of publicity, the young athletes in training, etc; another group drew a bowl of fruit, resting on a firm board, with a happy Kiwi picking away at the fruits. The first group drew attention to their athlete's slim waist, which they said represented a slim middle management; the second group had the narrow stem of the bowl representing the slender middle management connecting the strategic planners with the customer service people. You'll find that you can easily identify eight or ten key values which your ideal organization should have. Next steps: look at the drawings and ask: 'What's stopping us achieving these ideas right now?'

In every organization I have worked with, at least two-thirds of the factors stopping us achieving are within our own control. They have names like bureaucracy; tradition; 'the boss would never let us do it'; 'we tried it in nineteen-frozen-solid and it didn't work'; 'we'd never get it past the unions'; 'the middle managers resist change' (usually a much more accurate answer than the previous one); 'we're too busy coping with today's agenda to try doing new things for tomorrow'; 'that would require Department X to cooperate with Department Y, and we know they've been at daggers drawn'; 'we're in a monopoly position, so nobody can touch us', and so on. It really is rare for the external factors to be so overwhelming that they spell doom – and if they are, then the chances are that the organization has left it too late. The early signs of organizational failure are *always* internal; the problems come when the top management isolate themselves from employees at the customer interface, who are usually the ones who could tell them what's going on. How many managers do you know who never walk the floor, rarely come into contact with the customers, and spend all their time in their offices on the top floor reading reports? For a long time I worked with British Rail, as part of the ScotRail turnaround; we decided that it was time for our managers to experience the service from the customers' point of view, which meant selecting a group of them to make an ordinary journey – buying their own tickets, travelling second class, etc. One manager made a pained phone call: why should he buy a ticket, he asked, when he had a secretary to arrange passes? It's that sort of thinking which leads to a head-in-the-sand attitude, and isolates people from the truth that the future of the organization is much more in their hands than ever they might have believed.

Draw the ideal organization. It may be a customer-centred wheel, or a flower with each petal invested with meaning, or a fast car . . . whatever takes your fancy. The important point is that releasing the David in the organization means being prepared to talk values, metaphors, ideals, and beliefs. If you start from the organization chart, as so many people are tempted to do, then you're in the business of making adjustments from what you have now, making allowances for historical baggage, and the process inevitably becomes focused on making tolerable variations from the current situation. What you really need is the green-field vision of what the organization *should* be, followed by the hard look at the objections to being there – and then the realization that most of the objections are grounded in fears that are within our own control.

Maybe you don't feel that it's appropriate to start with the organization, or even your own part of the organization. Maybe you feel that it's better to start with *you*, the person within the marble overcoat of compromise and bureaucracy, the person who could do so much more if the organization came half-way to allowing it.

Reaching the David inside your own marble block is again a process driven by visions and metaphors. One term for it is 'guided imagery', where you consciously relax and take a walk through life as it has been and life as it might be. To do it properly, you need a little preparation:

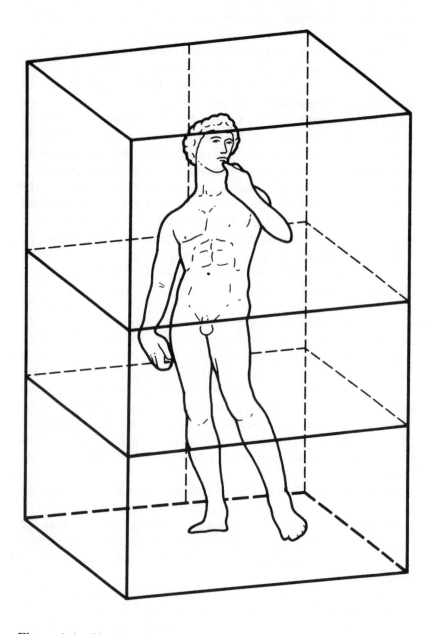

Figure 1.1   Naming the enemy

- a quiet place, preferably not your usual office or workplace, which might contain too many distractions
- time for the process to happen, at least an hour, probably a whole morning – it's not too much to devote to a process of transformation
- paper and pencil, and the willingness to produce drawings and scribbles as well as words and figures
- the willingness not to feel stupid when you talk to yourself out loud.

The purpose of the session is to help you revisit the ambitions and ideals you had when you began your working life; to help you identify the blocks and prohibitions which, for one reason or another, have stood in your way; to begin a plan to break out of them. On the next two pages you will find some prompting questions to think about; take the paper and pencil, chew over the questions, and – this is important – speak your thoughts out loud.

6 The David solution

When I started work . . .

I wanted to care for people

I wanted to make my mark

I wanted to invent something useful

I wanted to be a real craftsperson

I wanted to make good use of my education

I wanted to fulfil my parents' ambitions for me

I wanted to feel proud of the organization I work for

I wanted to be part of a good team

I wanted to find things out

I wanted to make a real difference

I wanted to do better than my peers

I wanted to please customers

I wanted to be independent

I wanted to take important decisions

I wanted to make money

I wanted to do something creative

I wanted to work at the leading edge

and whatever else occurs to you . . .

How often do I hear, or say . . .

We've never done it like that before (so we can't)

It's not in the manual/rule book

The unions/middle management would never accept it

I've got this bright idea, but nobody listens

We've commissioned a report on it

That's my department, so keep off

I don't know what the form's for, but Head Office wants it

I'm ashamed of what we give the customers

If Head Office wants the figures like that, Head Office
can have the figures like that (meaningless though they are)

You shouldn't have done that on your own initiative

It's not my fault – it's those people who need to change

What can you expect when I have staff like this?

All our problems would be solved by an injection of cash

This organization rewards the person who never makes a mistake

It's only a customer

and whatever else occurs to you . . .

Figure 1.1 is intended to represent the real you, trapped inside the block of organizational marble. Think about, say out loud, the component parts of the block. Do they have names like:

tradition
bureaucracy and the rule book
there's no prize for innovating
Head Office has all the power
we can't seem to work as a team
the bean-counters rule around here
my manager's more interested in building an empire
we tried it once and it didn't work
you've got to be a clone and toe the party line
Head Office is only interested in having forms filled in
there's no pay-off for starting change
there's a block at middle-manager level?

Read on. There are ways of dealing with all of these bugaboos. It's easier if you have help – colleagues who are equally committed and supportive. Some things are easier if you are a senior manager. But *anybody* can do things that stop the organization stifling itself and other people. We owe it to ourselves and others, to start. Now.

> The emperor had just moved into the palace. All around, he found good things; to his eyes, only one thing was missing. So, he summoned the gardener:
>
> 'These are beautiful gardens,' he said. 'There is only one suggestion I can make: that we have a double row of cedar trees from the eastern doors down to the lake.'
>
> 'Good heavens, your Majesty,' said the gardener. 'A double row of cedar trees will take a thousand years.'
>
> 'In that case,' said the Emperor, 'you'd better start this afternoon. We haven't a moment to lose.'

2   Starting

I was once invited to be the last of four speakers at a conference on organizational transformation; my topic was to be 'Busting the Bureaucracy'. I'd come with the prepared slides covering key points, and the store of amusing and tragic anecdotes; then just before I was due to speak my gorge rose, and I thought 'I don't want to do this, it's pointless'. So I spent the first ten minutes asking the audience to guess what I had on my slide of the ten key points. When they'd guessed eight of them, with no trouble, I asked whether they'd mind if we spent the rest of the time talking about why they didn't go ahead and do something about the bureaucracy, since they clearly knew as well as I did how to bust it.

This experience epitomizes the difficulty everybody has in taking the first steps in doing what's right. Whether it be giving up smoking, or taking up meditation, or deciding that *now* is the right time to start slashing at the tentacles of the bureacracy, there's always a hesitation: something has to hurt enough to make us finally do what we know is right.

One component of this reluctance is what I call the cookery book fallacy, because as a female who hasn't totally jettisoned sex-role stereotypes I recognize this one in myself. I have a large number of cookery books on my kitchen shelves, most of which I never cook from. They serve a purpose somewhere between dreaming and self-deception; I dream that I *could* cook a rijstaffel . . . I deceive myself that I *know how* to cook a rijstaffel . . . I could whip up a rijstaffel any time I want to, it's just not the right time . . . maybe I believe that I am an expert rijstaffel cook. Of course, I haven't ever cooked one, and my belief is therefore gained by reading rather than practice; but somehow I feel a better cook for having these pristine books on the shelves. And I stick to the three stained and battered monsters which have seen me through the last twenty years. Other people may find the same purpose is served by books on gardening, sex, or car maintenance.

You see the cookery book fallacy manifest in organizations when staff assemble to hear the latest guru deliver an inspirational speech, or watch the newest training video, or troop off to some overpriced seminar – and do nothing different with the message they've heard, but somehow kid themselves that they are better managers for having heard it. We have read Harvey-Jones or Iacocca; we've seen Tom Peters on video; we know some of the latest catch phrases. Improvement through osmosis: it doesn't work.

Quick test to see how much of the cookery book fallacy pervades your organization: what happens to people who return from training courses? Does their manager routinely de-brief them; give them an opportunity to share what they learned with the rest of the team; write the exercise of the new skills into the person's key result areas, or provide other opportunities for using them? How often do you and your colleagues send one another articles, clippings, *'thought you'd like to see this'* notes? Or on the other hand, how much have you spent on inspirational videos or fancy customer care courses, with little or no top management follow-up? How many seminars and conferences do you go to where afterwards you say the best part was meeting people from other organizations? Some of them, at least, should have sent you away equipped with new things to do.

Another story; one I heard years ago, and I still can't make up my mind whether it's the best piece of process consultancy I've heard or the biggest bit of bare-faced cheek. (The more I think about it, the more I incline to the former judgement.)

In the days when terms like Organization Development and Process Consultancy were relatively new, one of the great gurus was Chris Argyris. (Still is, actually.) A smallish British firm decided that it had a need for some Organization Development, whatever that was, and saved up its pennies to buy one whole day of Argyris's time. The entire board assembled to hear him speak.

Argyris took his seat, and was silent.

After a while, one of the board members stood up and began describing their problems. Argyris remained silent.

Another board member then began to speak. And another, and another . . but still nothing from Argyris. Soon the flip chart had been covered with words and diagrams, and everyone except Argyris was engaged in debate.

His silence continued over lunch. At three o'clock the managing director had finished an elaborate diagram of a current problem, and Argyris stood up, went to the flip chart, and picked up the magic marker left by the MD. A hushed silence fell on the group.

Argyris capped the magic marker, and as he replaced it in its trough said: 'You know, if you don't put the caps back on these things they dry up'. And that was the last thing he said.

At any rate, he was someone who wouldn't play the cookery book game.

Recently I worked with a group of people from the personnel function of a large company in dire trouble. We were working on a plan for the personnel department's contribution to getting the organization out of the mire. They worked hard and well, and put together a splendid presentation for the group personnel director's arrival on Friday. They had a plan to bust the bureaucracy, make innovation easier, get back in touch with the customer, reduce interdepartmental fights, give up a lot of their own power. It wouldn't have been the total salvation of the company, but it would surely have helped.

The personnel director sat through it all, and then responded: 'I can see the sense of what you say, and if you can prove to me now that it stands a 95 per cent chance of working, I'll give it serious consideration'. Thus demonstrating the low-risk, anti-innovation attitudes that had got them into trouble in the first place. They packed up, and started reading the job adverts in *The Daily Telegraph* and preparing their résumés.

Three weeks later the personnel director sent for me. I've never seen such a change in a person in so short a time. A month before, he'd had 200 staff; now he had twelve, and would shortly have four. All the power he had wielded had been delegated out to divisions (often to line managers). He pointed to the flip charts prepared in the workshop. 'Well,' he said, 'they got what they wanted.' He could have been on the team. He could have been part of it. But the new management (a well-known company doctor was now heading the organization) had cut him out of the process. In his head, he'd seen the logical arguments; but somehow his heart hadn't been able to respond in time.

That's the worst story I know. Here's the most courageous:

> The editor of *Cosmopolitan* magazine called together her senior staff one day. 'I have a secret for you,' she said. 'We're going to start another magazine: it'll be for the young liberated woman, with a career and an independent life-style, earning and spending well – definitely not the knitting patterns and nappies end of the market. Can you let me have your thoughts about the kind of features, advertising, etc., that we should put in it, within the next three weeks please?'
>
> She was deluged with suggestions. When the three weeks was up she called together the same group of people. 'I've got news for you,' she said. 'We already have a magazine for the young liberated woman, with a career and an independent life-style, earning and spending well – definitely not the knitting patterns and nappies end of the market. It's called *Cosmopolitan*. What I need to know now is – what happened, what did you do or I do, that stopped you bringing all these ideas to me before I made my announcement?'

Something has to hurt enough for us to act on our problems. I used to work for an organization where one director had a much clearer vision of the future than any of the others. I'd drop into his office for a chat, and he'd usually produce his latest paper to the board detailing his concerns, his ideas, his proposals. The problem was, none of them was ever accepted. They were brilliant analyses, but the rest of the board found them remarkably easy to turn down. He didn't understand why. I remembered the work of my old friend and colleague Neil Rackham, who's the world Number One on sales skills; in particular, Neil talking about why so many sales training courses concentrate on objection handling. 'That's because their early training sets them up to *create* objections,' said Neil, referring to the fact that most sales training courses encourage the salesperson to close before the prospect is ready. 'The unskilled salesperson will often move in on a need which *they* can see, but which the client doesn't feel. What the salesperson doesn't realize is that people are very good at living with their problems; if the salesperson tries to bully the client into purchasing, all this creates is objections. The skilled salesperson takes the problems which the client has so far been happy to live with, and by drawing out the implications of these problems makes them hurt enough for the client to want a solution. *Then* the salesperson asks for the order.' With his usual clear vision Neil had nailed the point, that most of us have a range of problems which we are content to live with. We know that the bathroom needs tiling, that we must give up smoking, we must do something about the insurance or fixing that rattle in the boot. Somehow the problem doesn't hurt enough for us to want to fix it. Neil's approach to sales training concentrates in helping the salesperson identify implication questions; the point of such a question is that it takes a tolerated problem (for example, the photocopier that's prone to go on the blink) and asks about all the other things that go wrong because of the defective copier – reports and proposals going out late, staff working overtime, work going to the local print shop, etc. When the tentacles of the problem are exposed, extending into many other operational areas the prospect hadn't thought of, there's a better basis for achieving commitment to a sale.

What has to hurt enough for *you* to take action on the marble blocks which emprison the empowered manager in the empowered organization? Some points to meditate upon (again, if you can speak rather than think you'll do better):

What is the worst thing that could happen
if I broke a silly rule? . . . and what's the best?

Who else would follow my example?

If we change, it doesn't necessarily mean that we were
wrong – just that yesterday's solutions are different from today's
Suppose I disbanded this committee that's doing nothing.

Take one or two customer complaints, and examine
the degree to which the problem – or the organization's response
to it – was hampered by the marble blocks. Now reflect on
the very small percentage of customers who bother to complain –
how many have just decided never to do business with you again?

If I start tomorrow, what sort of difference will I see
within a week – a month – a year?

The bean counters only have power because

(*a*) they are non-playing referees, and (*b*) we've allowed them
to take it. (For *bean counters* substitute *personnel*, or whoever is
the one-who-must-be-obeyed in your organization.)

Just one thing to do differently. Not the whole world –
just one thing.

How do I know that everyone else isn't waiting for
someone to set an example?

Make your case to (*a*) the new managing director
who's been brought in to save the organization,
(*b*) the customer/taxpayer/patient/claimant who wants
to know what you do for your money.

Think of the fun you could have

The best piece of advice I ever heard about the problem of starting came to me, age five, when I read the one and only Enid Blyton book I've ever had. (It was a birthday present from an aunt who didn't understand.) At some point in this book the heroine, a circus performer who rode zebras, was kidnapped by the bad man and tied up. As she struggled in despair, she remembered the advice of the escapologist, who'd let her into the secret of what to do when bound hand and foot and about to be dropped into a vat of boiling oil. 'You test the knots, one by one,' he said. 'There is always one knot that's easier than any of the others. This is the one you start with, and working on it frees the ones nearby, and so on.'

Start with the easiest knot, and start with just one knot. Transforming an organization, and reclaiming your own power-fulness, is not an overnight transformation, not a Lazarus job. It starts with doing one or two things differently – the things that are easiest to influence, the things within reach. It's what Peters and Waterman meant when they wrote about '*doing the doable*'. Don't wait for other people to make huge changes in order that you can throw in your twopennyworth; don't sit there dreaming about new legislation, or a change in the board, or a change in world economic conditions. Big changes are more likely to happen as a *result* of lots of small changes than they are to be their cause. Do what is sensible, what is within reach; and then the other knots will come free.

I was talking along these lines once with a group of managers, and I saw that one of them wasn't convinced. Questioning him further, I could see that his vision of the process was one of untying a hundred knots, one by one, each taking the same effort as the first. 'No,' I said, 'it's not like that. For every knot that you undo, you free at least two more: one by release, and one by example. By release? because you know that when you're unravelling string, no matter how horridly tangled it looks, in reality there are only a few key knots you have to concentrate on. Most loosen themselves once you've acted on the key knots. And by example? because there are other people who will see what you are doing, and follow. The process isn't linear, it's exponential.'

We talked about other useful strategies: if you're working on a whole organization, for example, then do a superb job for the Cinderella division (every organization has one) and make the rest jealous; go for some early visible successes – it's not always right to do good by stealth – and, if you can, arrange for customers and customer contact people to do your boasting for you, because theirs is the most powerful voice of all; keep a notebook of the situation, and your actions, against those grey days when you feel that nothing's going right and you need to remind yourself how dreadful it used to be. These are important supporting strategies. But the single message remains – the Enid Blyton contribution to management theory: look for the easiest knot, work on that one, feel the rest start to come free.

The next four chapters are dedicated to chipping away at some of the more common blocks of marble imprisoning the empowered manager: blocks like bureaucracy and tradition, paralysis by analysis, empire-building and the power of Head Office, the 'corporate concrete' problem that often lurks at middle manager level, etc. Then I'll look at some of the constructive ways in which people and organizations can bring about transformation: customer care, the enabling organization, teamwork, and trans-formational leadership. Finally there are some areas that ought to be on every manager's agenda: the issues of values and principles which I believe we will all soon be faced with.

3 Busting the bureaucracy

The single most insightful remark about bureaucracies was offered by Charles Handy, in his book *Understanding Organizations:*

> In a bureaucracy, it is more important that everybody performs to the same standard than that some people excel.

David won't come out of his marble prison for a promise like that.

The roots of bureaucracy go back to the time in an organization's life when some structure and order needed to be imposed otherwise nobody would know where they stood and what job they were supposed to be doing; to the time when the organization made the transition from its pioneering stage to the more stable state. Changing from a small, fast-moving, rapidly growing organization to one that is consolidating its success requires that some systems and procedures be brought in. It's not always easy for people who are drowning in bureaucracy to remember that there was a time when the systems and controls they grumble about now were the medicine the organization needed to help it survive. The problem is that after a while the systems and procedures acquire a life and power of their own, so that it feels as if the purpose of the organization is to please head office by following the rules. This problem is happening in many organizations right now; just as, fifteen or so years ago, most organizations were queueing up to buy ready-packaged systems and procedures (remember the rush for Management by Objectives? for performance appraisal systems that came ready to plug in?). Now most organizations of any size are looking for ways of busting those systems and procedures because they recognize that no longer are they a frame, they are a cage.

Unfortunately, busting the bureaucracy is a much harder task than adopting one. Bureaucracies are comfortable places to live, if you concentrate on conformity to the system and don't ask awkward questions like 'Are we losing touch with our customers?' and 'What have I done today that makes a real difference?' And I have to report here an inescapable fact, which I find distasteful but true. Told as a fable, it goes like this:

> Fresh out of college in, say, 1970 you apply to one of the large, successful organizations whose name is a household word for stability and success. As part of your early training you are familiarized with the policy and procedure manuals. You learn about important things like organization charts, job evaluation schemes, how much you can spend on your own authority, how to participate in committee meetings . . . and so you pick up, in these early days, the message that what you have to do to be good around here is learn to obey the rules and procedures. Maybe, the implicit message is, if you're good you'll become a middle manager and you can write some rules and procedures of your own.
>
> Twenty years on, you're a middle or senior manager. For the last twenty years you've been rewarded for obeying the rules. And now a bunch of young Turks come in talking about busting the bureaucracy, customer first, risk-taking, empowering junior managers, and all of that . . . how do you feel?

You feel rotten, of course. It's no secret that the most difficult group of people to engage in an organization transformation are the middle managers. They've been socialized to behave in a way that rewards them for knowing the rules, for solving problems by applying past experience, for playing safe. It isn't easy for them to make the transition.

I call this the 'corporate concrete' problem. What I find distasteful is that it smacks of what the Americans call ageism; also, it's easy to ignore the fact that the twenty years' hard work put in by today's corporate concrete enabled the organization to reach a stage of development where it can *afford* to say to them: 'Thanks, but now we need something different'. There are two inescapable realities: that the managers responsible for turning around organizations are typically a generation younger than the corporate concrete – most I know are in their late thirties or early forties – and that they are of a quite different psychological type from the corporate concrete. More on this in Chapter 5.

How does bureaucracy disable people? If you're stuck in the middle of one, this next bit may seem like watching an operation on television when you're writhing in agony yourself, but here nonetheless is a recital of symptoms:

Bureaucracy . . .

– encourages people to say 'I didn't do it because nobody told me I could,' or 'I didn't do it because it's not in the rule book'.

– judges and rewards people on their conformity to the prescribed processes, rather than on the outcomes of their activities.

– is more concerned with enforcing minimum standards of performance than rewarding excellence, so people feel that their mistakes are noticed far more than their successes.

– encourages the spirit where managers evaluate themselves on the size of the department or budget they control, and not on the impact of the work they do.

– thereby encourages interdepartmental rivalries and non-cooperation.

– encourages people to spend their energies giving the system the information it needs rather than reporting the true state of affairs, or outwitting the system because it stops them doing their job.

– encourages people to evaluate one another on their relative positions in the hierarchy, rather than on their contribution, and to collect status symbols.

– imposes the rule-book on customers, who then do their best to run away, and on staff, who then become involved in industrial relations disputes or feel they have no way of making their voice heard.

– demands proof in advance that innovations will be successful, thereby ensuring that little or no real innovation takes place.

And so on. Maybe one day someone will collect a book of bureaucracy stories and make a fortune; they might include the Frank Muir and Dennis Norden one about how they were pursued by the BBC for return of an overpaid fee, which of course they'd spent; eventually they procured some official-looking paper and wrote back that 'unfortunately, our computer system has no provision for returning money,' and never heard another word. I'll contribute the true story of what happened in the early days of the IBM performance appraisal system, when some bureaucrat ran wild and announced that each department's performance ratings would conform to the normal distribution curve. This is the kind of edict that causes immense problems, with managers forced to explain that they cannot grade their people the way they would like to because the number of ratings in each category has been prescribed by head office. In IBM in particular, few managers would care to admit to having D-grade performers (the lowest acceptable rating) working for them; so there were howls of protest from various parts of the system when this quota was imposed upon them. Except in IBM Germany, where most managers turned in perfect normal curves which had been attained in many cases by the transfer of poor performers from managers who had an over-supply to managers who lacked their quota; for a while, a spare D-grade performer was as good as money in the bank if you were talking to a manager who didn't have any. In *The Reckoning* David Halberstam tells the story of how thousands of perfectly good Ford spare parts were dumped in the river because head office was demanding inventory figures that took no account of the realities of the business.

Most people despairing of the bureaucracy can tell stories like that: how they take systems that are designed to facilitate the management of people, like performance appraisal or compensation and benefits, and turn them into systems for generating data for head office to play with; how they lead to faking the figures because it's easier to do that than to get the arch-bureaucrats to listen. Here follows a constructive suggestion:

At the top of every computer-generated report, every written statement from the field to head office and vice-versa, the following legend should be written:

THE MAP IS NOT THE TERRITORY

It might just help

Enough of wallowing in misery. I was tempted to put a little quiz in here, a sort of *'Test Your Bureaucracy Quotient'* with items in it like: *'Say the first things that come into your mind when you hear the following words: protocol, committee, procedure'* and *'If a bookworm, travelling at one inch per day, began to burrow through the procedure manuals in this organization, would it ever reach the other side given the rate at which new rules are being added?'* But I decided against it; when did you last meet a bureaucrat who was able to laugh at himself?

How do you set about busting the bureaucracy? Well, you won't do it overnight, and you'll probably never do it so completely that you can be sure it won't creep back. So the first thing to say to a would-be bureaucracy buster is that you must love the organization, or the ideals it stands (or used to stand) for, or the customers it serves. Because you're in for a hard time, and your rewards in the early stages won't come from the orthodox places; you'll be making trouble for the bosses, and your first warm fuzzies will come from customers, and from subordinates whose lives you've made easier. Can you cope with that? Then here's a check-list for action.

Break unhelpful rules

An unhelpful rule is one that stands in the way of good customer service, or teamwork within the organization, or innovation. You're challenging the fact that the bureaucracy evaluates you on the process, and you want to be evaluated on the outcome; so, if it's an important issue, you may want to keep the evidence. The tough thing is to have the courage to do it first time: ask yourself *'What's the worst thing they could do to me'* Almost certainly it won't be that bad.

Innovative variants on this theme are: looking for the really creative things that nobody's thought of forbidding, and rebellious conformity to the rules. These variations are best tackled by people who have a valuable place in the organization and maybe a reputation already as a bit of an *enfant terrible*; they can get you into trouble if you try them on your first day with a new employer. Two stories to illustrate:

> I moved into a position where I was managing a large number of weekly-paid staff. In those days there was no company sick pay; if you were ill you had to rely on state benefits, which were meagre. I called the whole group together and said that I was willing to pay sick employees their basic wage, provided that my total wage bill did not increase as a result, in other words I was asking colleagues to cover for the sick person. In doing this, I was actually exerting much tighter control over malingering than I could have done any other way, because the peer group would make sure that nobody was skiving. However, I got a rocket from the personnel department and the accountant. In vain did I protest that nowhere in the rule book was the practice forbidden. It lasted about six months – a good try.

> Readers of *Thomas the Tank Engine* will remember that the most important freight train was the Flying Kipper, which took the day's fish catch to London. One day, the station yardmaster, an officious brute, was walking through the sheds when he saw a man apparently doing nothing, and shouted at him to 'pick that ****ing broom up and start sweeping.' Obediently, the man did so. Later, control came on the phone, agitated: where was the driver for the Flying Kipper – it was late, and in danger of missing its path. Searches found the driver, still sweeping, innocently protesting that he was only obeying orders.

I particularly like 'rebellious conformity to the rules' as a strategy which can be applied by almost anyone in an organization; in a bull session on a workshop recently one of the participants described being had up on a charge of 'malicious obedience' during his army service. It's not enough by itself, it's only twisting the tiger's tail, and eventually someone has to pot the tiger between the eyes. But it's fun, and it keeps one's sense of identity, and maybe it wears the tiger out a bit.

Don't issue rules, issue principles

This is the other side of the first point. If you're a policy-maker, if you're someone who's expected to issue rules, try issuing principles instead.

Rules for converting a rule into a principle

1   Read the rule thoroughly, out loud, from beginning to end.
2   Close your eyes and say out loud, in simple English: 'What we are trying to achieve here is . . .' If necessary, imagine that you are being interviewed on radio and you have fifteen seconds to make your point to your interrogator.
3   Write down what you have just said.
4   If, despite step 2 above, any traces of the third person, passive voice, complex subordinate clauses, or other aids to obfuscation have crept in, eliminate them.
5   You now have a principle.

Rules talk about processes; principles about outcomes. Rules forbid; principles encourage. Rules are bound to leave some contingencies uncovered; principles do not. Rules specify that one way should be followed; principles leave room for ingenuity and for special circumstances.

Of course every organization needs some rules. There are duties of financial probity, public safety, and adherence to the laws of the land, which are rightly inescapable and can only be described by rules that are not to be deviated from. Problems arise when the rule-culture spreads into areas of the organization's life where it's not needed; when people become accustomed to making rules about everything, instead of asking how few rules they need to run the organization well. One participant in a workshop put it like this: 'The boss should go through every rule in the book, and preface it with the phrase "I do not trust you, therefore . . ." Then s/he should think about how that rule comes across to the person reading it, and ask what the person feels like. And then s/he should think about how many rules need to remain.' He was giving clear voice to the lack of trust, the feeling of disempowerment and removal of initiative, that comes to any half-way intelligent person when they're told that the way we do things around here is to follow the rule book.

And how many rules could you do without, I wonder?

When the guru sat down to worship each evening, the ashram cat would get in the way and distract the worshippers. So he ordered that the cat be tied during evening worship.

Long after the guru died, the cat continued to be tied during evening worship. And when the cat eventually died, another cat was brought to the ashram so that it could be duly tied during evening worship.

Centuries later, learned treatises were written by the guru's disciples on the need for a bound cat in all properly conducted worship.

Replace central control by local authority

As long as the control of an organization resides in the centre, that organization is a bureaucracy.

There is one book which has never left my desk since the moment it was given to me. If I could give a copy to every manager I meet, I'd be content with that day's work. It's about an organization turnaround in which, amongst many other things, the boss took the philosophy of decentralization to its logical extreme and restructured the company so that workers elected their managers – and could fire them. The basis for the decision is very simple; if the workers wanted to do a good job (and how creatively the boss tried to establish a climate in which they *would* want to do a good job!) then the task of the manager was to create the conditions in which they could perform well. Nobody would know better than the workers whether or not the manager was doing a good job; therefore, the manager should be answerable to the workers, rather than the other way around. Apart from a few specialists recruited by other means, the whole organization pyramid was turned on its head: workers chose their managers, who chose *their* managers. Combined as it was with extraordinary leadership from the man at the top, the Cashbuild story is a real lesson in what can be achieved if one is prepared to re-think the organization from first principles.

The story is even more remarkable because it is set in South Africa, where many of the shopfloor workers were black and many of the managers, to start with at least, were white. The boss is Albert Koopman, and he wrote the story with two co-authors, Nasser and Nel, in a book called *The Corporate Crusaders*. I'll quote from it again before this book is finished, because it's a truly inspiring story.

Push authority as far down the organizational pyramid as you can. Koopman pushed it so far down that the organization turned topsy-turvy, and it went from R600,000 profits in 1982 to

R5,200,000 in 1987. If you don't feel like taking that big a risk, or it's not in your hands to do so, then at least push authority down to the level of the 'pivotal job' within your organization or your team.

And how do you tell where the pivotal jobs are? The pivotal jobs in the organization are the ones where the most impact, per jobholder, is made on the customers' perception of the organization. They may be customer contact jobs, or they may lie one or two steps up the organization, at the level where people take decisions about the situations the customer contact people will have to deal with and the resources they will have at their command. In big organizations you may also identify one or two other important levels of pivotal job, where for a relatively small expenditure of energy people have a great impact on customer perceptions and organization performance.

Now that you've identified the pivotal jobs, start looking at their functions through the eyes of the customer. One good strategy is to take a customer complaint, or a customer who doesn't fit the standard pro-forma. A common problem in bureaucratic organizations is that customer complaints take ages to deal with, because those in pivotal jobs don't have the authority to take decisions about the customer's needs, so matters have to be referred higher. Yet we all know from our experience as customers that the *speed* with which a complaint is acted on, or a decision taken, is often more important than the eventual resolution of the issue. So, start by asking 'How much authority would I have to delegate to enable the people in pivotal jobs to deal with 80 per cent of customer complaints, or difficult customer situations, without reference to higher authority?' Then go right ahead and delegate it. If necessary you can build in some checks (the 'micrometer slice' checks covered in Chapter 8 on enabling systems) to ensure that the authority isn't being abused.

The chances are that by making the 80 per cent cut-off rule you will have (*a*) made a significant, positive difference to the way customers and staff feel about the organization, (*b*) saved the work of a good many checkers and paper-pushers, and (*c*) cost yourself very little in terms of resources. For example, when we started work on customer care in British Rail we gave local managers the freedom to settle on the spot claims up to £100 for things like clothes soiled by dirty carriages, and refunds for unused tickets. It saved money; gave us a better relationship with the customers, and incidentally helped bring about a situation where local managers took more interest in carriage cleaning because the refunds for poor performance came out of *their* own budget.

In this example, I've examined the trade-off between speed of response and conformity of response. There are other trade-offs you can look at, using the same principle, always with customer service as the reference point: for example, there may be a trade-off between having customers seen by a variety of specialists versus them having a relationship with just one person; there may be a trade-off between managers having local systems they've designed themselves (and are therefore more likely to feel commitment to) and having them use a common system which makes for easier management of the overall organization at, perhaps, the cost of local commitment and sensitivity to local needs. The 80 per cent figure – how much authority would I have to delegate to allow people in the pivotal jobs to handle 80 per cent of the issues themselves – is based on the Pareto analysis that 20 per cent of the problems cause 80 per cent of the hassle; so, you delegate the hassle-free 80 per cent to those in the pivotal jobs, and save the checking, decision-making, debates about points of principle, for where it's actually needed.

All the above sounds too much like rules. Instead, here's a principle:

> The Catholic Church has the best organization structure in the world. Every Catholic knows his or her local priest; the local bishop; and the Pope. That's all they need to know; there is no need to come into contact with the rest of ecclesiastical hierarchy.

I wish I could remember who said that.

Introduce enabling systems

What's to replace the bureaucracy? Anarchy? People running around like headless chickens, all doing their own thing?

No. A large organization needs some systems and procedures. People have to be paid, goods bought, the tax authorities given the information and money they demand. The debureaucratized organization has systems and procedures which are enabling or empowering rather than controlling. Like decentralization, this concept is important enough to merit its own chapter; I only need to acknowledge here that the opposite of bureaucracy is not anarchy, but a redirection of the controls so that they form a framework rather than a cage. Just as, on a micro-level, you replace rules by principles, on a macro-level you replace the controlling systems by systems which support rather than restrict; which give people not a ceiling above which it is difficult to rise, but a floor below which they have no excuse for falling.

Enabling systems in operation are not neat. You can't describe them in a flow chart of procedures, because they don't seek to prescribe everything a person should do. Nor are they stable over time, because they are designed for an organization in which change is an accepted part of the process.

Take together all four principles for busting the bureaucracy – breaking unhelpful rules, issuing principles rather than rules, replacing central control by local authority, and introducing enabling systems – and it's obvious that the bureaucracy-buster is considerably increasing the amount of uncertainty in the organization. Here's a simple example: once you've decentralized control, the chances are that a manager in branch A will take a different decision from his counterpart in branch B in what may appear to be similar circumstances. How much does that bother you? Will you be prepared, say, to defend it to the media, if a journalist with nothing better to do asks why Mrs Barton in Newcastle received a cash refund on her defective holiday but Mr Hurst in Ipswich only got a voucher for money off his next one? In a debureaucratized organization, people have responsibility for their own decisions; they can no longer rely on the next level up to check their work and take their decisions for them. The certainty that someone else will share the responsibility is no longer there, and that's not always comfortable; after all, shared responsibility is nobody's responsibility. Helping people through that discomfort is a hearts-and-minds matter. You can't bust the bureaucracy from behind a desk. You have to go out, be visible, offer real personal support to the people who are struggling with the new way of doing things. More about this in Chapter 9. And you have to be prepared to face the fact that although you may not be fired for busting the bureaucracy – most real bureaucracies only fire people if they're (*a*) very junior, (*b*) a public embarrassment, or (*c*) guilty of gross moral turpitude – you may not be the most popular pig in the synagogue either. So pick your battles carefully, think about the easiest knots, recruit support, make sure your successes are played up. And remember that the process itself, like all processes of organization transformation, looks like a hysteresis curve (you drew them in elementary physics, when you watched the rate at which magnetized iron filings fell into line – first a few, slowly, then a great rush, and finally the last coming slowly into line).

How do you know if you're succeeding in busting the bureaucracy? After all, it is a slow process, and it always feels like two steps forward and one step back. Here's a quick checklist:

We are successfully busting the bureaucracy when we have *less*:

- people asking the boss's permission to take decisions
- defensive paperwork
- obvious use of status symbols
- head office or middle management time spent checking decisions rather than making them
- proliferation of rules and rule-books
- cooking the books to please head office
- people keeping independent records to keep themselves in touch with what's really going on
- having to go 'through channels' to communicate with the person you need to talk to.

And we are successfully busting the bureaucracy when we have *more*:

- people making decisions and then telling the boss
- communication face-to-face or by telephone
- esteeming people on contribution rather than status
- tolerance of diversity of decisions in small (and, eventually, medium-sized) matters
- principles replacing rules as guidance for conduct
- principles of 'how little do we need to control' rather than controlling everything
- senior management being informally visible and approachable rather than relying on the printed word
- people saying that they now feel trusted.

4 Paralysis by analysis

One reason why David stays locked in his marble block is that the Old Guard prefer to spend all their time analysing the nature of the marble to three decimal places, seeing how it compares with the next door's marble, and calling for five competitive quotes on the hammer and chisel.

In so many organizations, the first response to a problem is to commission a report; put together a working party, call in the consultants, assemble a task force. In practice this is often the *only* response: the report sits on a shelf somewhere, never to be implemented. Those who commissioned it feel a sense of achievement because now they know what the problem is. The people who worked on uncovering the problem may have a slight sense of frustration because now they'd like to go ahead and do something about it, unless they've been in the organization long enough to know that 90 per cent of reports are in fact shelved. When the UK National Health Service was encouraged by the Griffiths Report to become more customer conscious, there was hardly a hospital in the country without a team of questionnaire-wielding investigators recording the clients' opinions of every aspect of the service. You could sense the feeling of 'Oh gosh, what do we do with it now?' coming over the teams as they finished delineating the problems; and the proportion of studies that actually led to action was probably about one in ten. The move from analysis to action doesn't happen automatically; X-raying the block of marble doesn't cause David to emerge from it; knowing the problem by its long name doesn't necessarily cause you to start solving it. The situation is called paralysis by analysis; at its worst, it combines a gratifying feeling of being very busy with a comfortable belief that the problem is within one's grasp, while contributing absolutely nothing at all to its solution.

Measuring rather than understanding

I remember as a student of psychology being amazed at the fact that the British had devoted an enormous amount of effort to the *measuring* of intelligence at various stages of a child's growth, but it had taken a Swiss psychologist, Piaget, to describe the *development* of intelligence in the growing infant. Our own prescribed studies reflected this preference for measurement rather than understanding: we spent hours of classroom time studying tests of intelligence, and how the measurements were calculated; Piaget's work was relegated to an optional two hours of supplementary reading, and never featured in our examinations. It appears to be an integral part of the Anglo-Saxon intellectual tradition to prefer measuring things to understanding them or, worse, to kid ourselves that once we have measured things we *have* understood them. Once alerted to this preference, you can see it at work in so many supposed problem-solving activities: they stop at problem description, they regurgitate figures, sometimes they quarrel about new ways of presenting figures, but they don't run the data through the brain and ask '*What's really going on here*?'

The poet Roy Campbell, writing about some modern critics, expressed it well:

> You praise the firm restraint with which they write;
> I'm with you there of course,
> They use the snaffle and the curb all right,
> But where's the bloody horse?

Better a late certainty than a timely approximation

This preference for measurement rather than understanding, let alone action, is reinforced by the legacy left to so many organizations by the rule of the bean counters. Writing about the decline of the American car industry, David Halberstam in his book *The Reckoning* quotes the clashes between the manufacturing men, typified by Iacocca, and the finance men in Ford when things were starting to crumble: how the finance men, conditioned by their MBA training to analyse situations to the last percentage point, would delay decisions to wait for more data, while the manufacturing men were saying that they'd rather make a decision now, on 70 per cent of the data, than wait six months for the rest of the data to come in by which time naturally the situation would have changed. Of course, in Ford as in so many ailing organizations, the reins of power had passed from the innovators to the bean counters; so no matter how much the manufacturing side protested, the winners were the finance people.

There is enormous safety in the late-but-exact game; the participants are protected from having to correct their mistakes, because they can safely protest that the data are now out of date, and what's the point of crying over spilt milk, and yes, the performance indicators for January did look dreadful, but it's now June and we should be looking to the future and not indulging in post-mortems and the blaming game. Any prescription for organization transformation includes the introduction of simple performance indicators that bring data on current performance to the attention of the people who must act on them *in time to correct errors and capitalize on successes*. Achieving this means that the top priority is to pass information to the people closest to the coal-face, rather than to the folk in head office; and establish an expectation that they don't just receive the information, they act on it.

We're far too cerebral

Another reason why paralysis by analysis is so common is that we in the Western world are so cerebral, so oriented towards words and numbers and flow-charts, that we come to believe that if we can't describe something with mathematical precision it doesn't exist. Sometimes thi leads to concentrating on the details rather than the big picture; sometimes it leads to inability to concentrate on anything at all. When management by objectives was introduced, many organizations encouraged the view that an objective was only an objective if you could measure it to two decimal places; leading of course to far too much focus on the figures and not enough on qualitative issues. Remember the brief vogue for human asset accounting – a doomed attempt to treat human beings, with all their diversity, perversity, creativity, and variety, as if they were inventory on a shelf or items to write, seriously, into the balance sheet?

> In old Bohemia, the peasants used to drive their pigs to market for sale. In the centre of the market-place there was a large plank centred over a log, like a see-saw. The pig would be coerced into sitting on one end of the plank, while its owners scoured the market place for a stone that would exactly balance the weight of the pig.
> Then they guessed the weight of the stone.

It's no accident that many of the techniques designed to allow people's creativity to flow freely, mind mapping and guided imagery for instance, rely on breaking the spell of words and figures and critical comment. The language of creativity is the language of metaphor – vision, pattern, image, *Gestalt*, picture – rather than the language of analysis and criticism; when we review our own creative achievement we think about feelings, excitement, joy, frustration. When Michelangelo was envisioning David, I doubt very much that he thought about the exact weight in marble required to complete the job; nor did he have his time manager in one pocket and his copy of *The One-Minute Sculptor* in the other.

The naming fallacy

Add to these reasons two more: the naming fallacy, and the cookery book fallacy. I described the cookery book fallacy in Chapter 2 on starting: the feeling that just having read the recipe makes one a better cook, or having listened to the guru makes one a better manager, all without ever moving into the heat of the kitchen. The naming fallacy is at the root of the feeling we all have when we go to the doctor with an undiagnosed malady and the doctor says that's a Wilkinson's fracture, or a bad case

of coriolanus; the little frisson of relief that the problem has a
name, is recognizable by an expert, we haven't been imagining it.
Honest doctors will sometimes admit that many a disease has been
'cured' by giving it a name, saying that there's a lot of it about, and
providing a bottle of nasty-looking medicine. This doesn't work
so well with organizations, though, even when doctor and patient
connive in the fallacy.

> The frog was drowning in quicksand. As he was going down for the
> third time, he looked up to see an owl perched on the branch of a
> tree above him. The owl was wearing a T-shirt bearing the name of
> a well-known firm of consultants.
> 'Help, help,' cried the frog, 'I'm drowning!'
> The owl looked down and contemplated the frog. The frog cried out
> some more.
> 'Do you really want my help?' asked the owl. The frog gasped that
> of course he did. 'It'll cost you,' said the owl. 'I don't care,' said the
> frog, 'I'm drowning!'
> The owl stroked his beard for a while, and then cleared his throat.
> 'My advice to you, frog, is that you should learn to fly.'
> 'How on earth can I learn to fly when I'm drowning in this
> quicksand?' cried the frog.
> 'We at McAllen's do not concern ourselves with the implementation
> of our recommendations,' said the owl, loftily, writing out his fee
> account.

It's worth looking at the reports you've commissioned or contrib-
uted to and at the ratio of description of problem to recommendations for action. In my experience it's between 4:1 and 8:1, and
would lose nothing by being cut to somewhere between 2:1 and
4:1; the remainder of the description is there to assure whoever
commissioned the study that the doers did gather some data. And
I don't just mean the large-scale reports and major studies; look at
the average performance appraisal form, for example, and you'll
probably see a similar ratio between description of problem and
recommendation for action, as if all that had to be done was to
call the problem by name for it to lose its power.

How do we break out of it?

The task is two-fold: to present our own thoughts, analyses,
recommendations in such a way that our hearers feel compelled

to act; and to recognize and suppress within ourselves the tendency to believe that once we've identified the problem we've solved it. Analyses that don't lead to paralysis but to action:

1   Never hide behind the impersonal or the passive.
2   Put the statistics at the back.
3   Aren't stuffed full of footnotes and references to show that the writer is well-read.
4   Build bridges between those commissioning and those who contribute.
5   Make the problem hurt by spelling out the implications.
6   Use a good deal of 'And this means that . . .'
7   Identify actions with individual people, not impersonal functions or bodies.
8   Meet the 'what's s/he going to do for you then?' test.
9   Are 'Yesable'.
10 Are delivered personally and followed up.

Never hide behind the impersonal or the passive

This advice probably contradicts all the formal report-writing courses you've ever been on. Nonetheless I stand by it, because it prevents, at one stroke, the kind of dissimulation and fudgery that makes it easy for people to shrug off responsibility for opinions, decisions, information. Get rid of all the 'It was felt that . . .' and 'It became apparent that . . .' and 'The view of the manufacturing department was . . .' and replace it by 'I feel that, we feel that . . . I saw, we saw . . ., the manufacturing director said . . . .' Put your money where your mouth is. Stand by your findings and opinions. Unless you've promised people anonymity, name them. Taken with point 7, you'll find that this style of writing reports helps you be precise about what you discovered and what you want to have happen. I remember seeing a similar principle at work when I presented my little book on performance appraisal systems to Malcolm Stern, my editor at Gower Publishing. With the traces of my academic background still fresh, I'd given it a sub-title: 'The design, installation, and maintenance of performance appraisal systems'. Quietly Malcolm took his pen and re-wrote it: 'Designing, installing, and maintaining performance appraisal systems'. Thanks, Malcolm.

Put the statistics at the back

I'm not anti-statistics, far from it. Many reports need statistics to support them. The principle behind this point is simply one of thinking what your reader is going to be doing when s/he's reading your report. Ten to one, s/he'll be reading it on the train home, in the back of the chauffeur-driven car, or over a sandwich lunch. If you're unlucky, s/he'll be covertly reading it behind the clip board during the reading of the minutes of the previous meeting. You therefore have to assume that (*a*) the reading will be interrupted, and (*b*) your reader may not finish it. Therefore, make your main points as a compelling narrative text, as the first part of the document. Leave the statistics, and descriptions of the complicated techniques you used, for the appendix. You don't want anything in the body of the proposal to interfere with the flow of your narrative; like it or not, statistical tables do just that.

Aren't stuffed full of footnotes and references to show that the writer is well-read.

This is a fault which people from academic backgrounds are particularly prone to; feeling that it's not OK to say anything substantial unless you can back it up with notes and references. It has no place anywhere else. As a student, you do the fancy stuff with the references (*a*) to prove to your tutor that you haven't spent all your time in the students' union, but have at least passed through the library, and (*b*) to allow other researchers to look up for themselves the work on which you based yours. Once you're in business, you have to accept that these factors no longer operate. If someone's asked you to do an investigation, it's because they trust your judgement, not your academic qualifications. If you're putting a proposal of your own, then *you* have to trust your judgement. If you need some supporting evidence, then accept that nobody's going to look it up; it goes, photocopied, as an appendix.

Build bridges between those commissioning and those who contribute

If you're asked to survey the customers, part of your task is to help your sponsor hear what the customers have to say. If you're asked to design the employee attitude survey, part of your task is to take to top management the voice of the employees as if it were a responsibility they had delegated to you. If you're making the corporate video showing the way ahead, you are charged with helping the listeners get on all fours with the speakers. Some of it is more like good journalism, good reportage, than the bald presentation of abstract data. Empathy is as important as analysis.

Make the problem hurt by spelling out the implications

This point was mentioned in Chapter 2 on Starting: the need to take a problem that people are, on the evidence, content to live with, and show how it has implications for the rest of the operation that should make it less tolerable. If, for example, you wanted to make a case for delegating more authority to local managers, your primary case might rest on cost savings and the fact that nearly everyone else is doing it. But you stand more chance if you can point out some of the other things that happen when managers are disempowered: reluctance to innovate, detachment from the need to behave cost-effectively because the decisions are out of their hands, slow or inappropriate responses from head office support functions, central decisions which are inappropriate to local needs . . . with whatever supporting evidence you can muster. You have to assume that your auditors all have, at home, the untiled bathroom and unserviced lawn mower which they know they should do something about; you are the unexpected guest or early spring which will force them to do something about it, now.

Use a good deal of 'And this means that . . .'

By which I mean that it's easy to become so immersed in your data that, consciously or unconsciously, you think the recommendations for action are so obvious that you'd be insulting the reader's intelligence by pointing them out.

They are obvious to you, because you've lived with the information for days or weeks. You've locked yourself away somewhere undisturbable so that you can put your presentation together. You're ready to answer on the spot when the marketing director wants to know whether there are regional differences and the personnel director asks whether there's any connection with length of service. If you're a natural change agent, you're probably the kind of person who automatically looks at the world in terms of what you have to do next. It's important to remember that your listeners and readers are not as familiar with the implications as you are, nor may they be so change-oriented; they *need* you to spell out for them what it is you want to happen. An excellent discipline to follow is to go through your presentation and for each problem or issue that you have highlighted, start a sentence in your mind beginning with 'And this means that . . ..' If you can't complete the sentence, maybe the point isn't a real one; if you can complete the sentence, leave the point as a trigger for action.

Identify actions with individual people, not impersonal functions or bodies

Dispense with any sentence that begins 'Management must . . .' or 'It is for individual departments to decide . . .' or 'We shall discuss with the unions . . ..' Like the use of the impersonal style, it's fudgery, it's hiding from responsibility. It gives no one person or persons the clear task of picking up the issues and doing something with them. Following this rule will clarify your own thinking: who, exactly in *management* are the people you want to see doing things better? If you can't name them, go away and think again.

A good little bit of self-discipline is the video test which works as follows. Ask yourself the question 'If my proposal gets accepted, and we want to make a video of people doing things differently as a result, what, exactly, are we going to show?' Take this one too far and you run the risk of over-concreting the issue, but before you've gone too far you'll have travelled some very useful bits of road.

I use the video test to great effect in workshops on empowering junior managers. I'm working with senior managers at the stage when they can admit that in theory it makes sense to release some power from head office. I ask them to write on flip charts some of the things they would expect junior managers to be doing differently. Usually they come up with global abstract words like 'decision-taking', 'accepting responsibility', 'autonomy', and so on. Then we do the video test: what decisions? responsibility for what? autonomy in what? Will we for instance be videoing these managers recruiting their own staff? firing staff? spending money on their own authority? stopping the line because of poor quality? Then we're really into what empowerment means.

Meet the 'what's s/he going to do for you then?' test

This one is very simple. You have presented your earth-shattering recommendations to the 'director in charge of certain things'. S/he's listened, given you coffee, fixed the date of the next meeting, upped your budget. As you leave the office, one of the DCCT's colleagues walks in and asks *'What's s/he going to do for you then?'* If you've done your job, the DCCT can, in a couple of sentences, answer the question. And the way you ensure that the DCCT can do this is by summarizing: during the proposal, at the end of the meeting, and – crucially – in no more than two paragraphs at the front of whatever document you prepare.

Are 'Yesable'

This doesn't mean that they're acceptable. It means that your proposals are sufficiently finished and fluent that, should your listener say *'Yes, go right ahead, now'*, you can do just that. I don't mean that you've invested in a thousand glaciers poised ready to roll over Africa (acknowledgements to *The Hitch-Hiker's Guide to the Galaxy*); it does mean that you know which buttons to press to make things happen. Of course, if you've hidden behind impersonal phrases and the passive voice you'll find this difficult; all the more reason to avoid them.

Not that it's always easy for the other person to give a straight 'Yes'. I treasure Colin Hogg, my first sponsor in British Rail; he'd asked me for a proposal, I'd set aside two hours for the meeting, I was sure he'd want to embroider it and leave his mark even though it was as yesable as I could make it. I was out of his office in fifteen minutes with a straight 'Yes', and I've often wished that there were more like him.

Are delivered personally and followed up

Do you read everything that lands on your desk? Do you remember it all with the same clarity as you remember face-to-face meetings? Or do you put some of it aside with the thought '*That's a good idea, I must get around to it some time*'? Of course you do, and so does the person you're trying to persuade. Try to deliver your thoughts face-to-face, or make a meeting to discuss them. Ring the people at the meeting and ask them how their ruminations are progressing. Cato the Elder, a Roman senator who understood these things, had a grudge against Carthage; every speech he gave in the Senate he ended with the phrase *Carthago delenda est* (Carthage must be destroyed). Eventually, his fellow-senators gave him his way.

And how do we avoid falling into the paralysis by analysis trap ourselves? We can of course try to insist that anyone wanting our ear obeys the previous ten commandments; but the other half is self-analysis and self-discipline. Here are some topics for meditation.

What's stopping me acting?

- Am I afraid of being punished for innovation?
- Am I afraid of apparently admitting past mistakes?
- When did I last disband a committee because it had run out of useful things to contribute?
- Is everybody (including me) waiting for someone else to be the first to start?
- Have I fallen for the 'cookery book fallacy': that because I have the recipe on my shelf I've as good as cooked the dish?
- Have I concentrated on the extra work implied, and not looked at the extra benefits?
- Am I playing the power game: that as long as I withhold consent I have more power than after I've given it?
- Am I picking and criticizing because I want to leave my mark on the proposal?
- What are the corporate 'if only we'd done something at the time' occasions of remembered pain? Have we learned enough to recognize whether this is another one in the making?
- What has to hurt enough to make me act, and how can I be sure that it isn't already hurting.

What's known, familiar, manageable, is so often preferable to the unknown and unfamiliar. Doing things is more visible than not doing things. The small print can always be argued with – to the point, if you're lucky, when the original ideas are now out of date.

But, I promise you, tomorrow won't be like that. Tomorrow is the day of the transformational leader. Robert Kennedy was fond of quoting: 'Some people look at things and ask Why? I look at things and ask Why not?' Paralysis by analysis will lead, inexorably, to death.

A man went to his doctor and complained of severe occupational stress.

'Tell me about your job,' said the doctor.

'I'm a tomato grader,' said the man. 'All day I sit at the end of a line and sort tomatoes into first grade, second grade, and rejects.

'What's so stressful about that?' asked the doctor.

'Well, it's decisions, decisions, decisions, all the time.'

5 Cracking the corporate concrete

Working as I do in the area of organization transformation, I find that I can achieve a totally undeserved reputation for prescience merely by remarking that most of the resistance comes from middle managers. 'How did you know that?' they ask. Because it's a worldwide phenomenon, that's how.

In some organizations the response has been to fire or otherwise disable all managers above a certain age. This is a pity; it's a blanket solution, and often a dishonourable one too. In my view, it's important to look at how the problem of the 'corporate concrete' at middle-manager level comes about, because that will (a) enable us to do something more sensitive about it, and (b) avoid its likely recurrence, albeit in a new overcoat, in a few years time.

The corporate concrete problem is the result of an interaction between two factors: the common pattern of organization growth and change; and the kind of behaviour which is rewarded, and the kind of people who are recruited, at a particular stage of organization growth.

In the appendix to this book (p.144), I've presented my model of organization growth and change. It's a three-stage model, showing the *pioneering* stage, which is characterized by informal organization, reactive management, rapid change, and lack of

41

specialization. As the organization grows, it gets to a size which requires systems and controls to make life more structured, organized, predictable; to ensure coherence, equity, and everyone knowing where they stand. In other words, this is the time when the organization needs formal policies and procedures, rule books, organization charts, management by objectives systems, and so on. They're the medicine it needs to su vive.

If the organization continues to grow, it reaches the stage where the systems and controls seem to have become the reason for the organization's existence. The whole place is being run for the benefit of head office; we don't do anything unless it's sanctioned by the policy manual; hierarchy and positional authority matter far too much. This is the *systems crisis*, and a great many organizations are in it right now, or struggling to get out of it. The way out is into the *integrated* stage, characterized by decentralization, bureaucracy-busting, shortening lines of authority, greater encouragement of innovation and risk-taking, and the transformational leadership and re-emergence of values which I will come to later.

If you think about it, the kind of behaviour which is rewarded in the systems stage is based on understanding and conforming to the rules. I remember working for IBM in 1970; one of the earliest gifts they gave me was the manager's manual. It contained, amongst other things, the guidelines on how much you could spend sending flowers to the spouse of an employee who had died on company service; there were three different amounts corresponding to grade, and suggested letters of sympathy. Of course, without such guidance one would never have thought of it for oneself . . .. In that same organization, the self-teaching manager's manual contained pages and pages of sample questions and answers: what should I do if one of my staff asks about his or her career prospects; whether they should join a union; want to know about the way their salary is calculated. You learned the answers parrot-fashion, and thus passed into the rarified realms of management.

I sometimes regret that we have little or no sense of organizational history. Heaven forbid the invention of yet another abstract academic discipline, but I often feel that a thorough look at the patterns visible in organizations, worldwide, might prevent us from falling into the trap of 'those who cannot remember the past are condemned to repeat it'. I'm sure that such a concentrated look would support the view that in the Western world, at least, many organizations passed into the systems stage at about the same time – the early 1960s to late 1970s. Industry in the West at that time was thoroughly recovered from the Second World War and resulting shortages: we entered instead into the affluent society. Terms like 'multinational', and 'the military-industrial complex', became commonplace. Those were the days when Harold Wilson's government introduced George Brown's National Plan, and Stafford Beer was putting the Chilean economy under central control with the help of the then new technology; later Edward Heath created the super-ministries; the French became even more enamoured of their own forms of *dirigisme*; and the USA introduced management by objectives (i.e. body count) into the conduct of warfare. Organizationally, it was when every second consultant was offering systems and procedures for regularizing the conduct of the organization – management by objectives, organization charts, performance appraisal systems, manpower and salary planning, corporate planning – the whole orientation was towards stability and predictability. In the process, various assumptions were made (usually without being spelled out or even recognized): that head office, and in particular the chief executive, knew best, and the function of the rest of the organization was to carry out their wishes; therefore, that communication *downwards*, to employees and customers, was more important than communication upwards; that uniformity of systems and procedures was more important than sensitivity to local needs (even when that uniformity was imposed across the totality of the newly-formed conglomerates, of which one component could be making windows and another part liquorice allsorts); that there were more and more areas in which line managers needed specialist help or should cede their responsibilities completely to specialist functions; and, crucially, that tomorrow would be the same as yesterday, or if different it would be different by degrees, not by qualitative change.

If this was the message, implicit and explicit, that was delivered to people starting their careers at that time, think about what's happened since then. If they weren't at home in such an atmosphere, then they either (*a*) didn't join, or (*b*) left to go elsewhere. If they were at home, they stayed. Got older. Were promoted. And now, fifteen or twenty or twenty-five years on, they are the

middle and senior managers who are resisting the changes that
need to happen if the organization is to survive into the third stage
of its growth.

Before we blame them, look at it from their point of view.
All their working lives they have been taught that this is the
way you manage a big organization, by stabilizing, formalizing,
regulating. Often it's because they were good at these things that
the organization has reached the stage it has. And now, late in life,
they are being told that someone's moved the goalposts. It's not
necessarily bloody-mindedness that makes them oppose change;
it's a lifetime of habit, reward, expectation, and motivation,
reinforcing the kind of people they were in the first place.
And, there's a lot of them about; in my own work using a
particular psychological test (the Myers-Briggs Type Indicator)
which is especially useful at identifying this kind of personality,
I've found as many as 85 per cent of middle and senior managers
conforming to this type; and others have found the same.

At the risk of considerable over-simplification, I shall describe
in more detail some of the psychological characteristics of people
who are typically at home in situations where the ability to manage
the stable state is valued.

Their style is that of the traditionalist, stabilizer, and
consolidator; they concentrate on the organization as an entity
in its own right and are capable of intense loyalty to it, expecting, of
course, that the organization will show loyalty in return. (This is one
reason why they often seem to be unnecessarily upset when offered
voluntary redundancy, even on apparently irresistible terms. They
see the organization as having broken an important psychological
contract.) Their abilities in establishing policies, rules, schedules,
routines, regulations, and hierarchy make a significant contribution
to bringing order into chaos, which is why they tend to find
themselves in the jobs they do. They are good at setting up
lines of communication and at following things through; usually
patient, thorough, steady, reliable, and orderly. They place a high
value on policies, contracts, and standard operating procedures;
they carefully preserve the traditions of the organization, and
should they not exist, are likely to be the ones to create them.
Often they have a special sense of social responsibility and are
pillars of their local communities; they are industrious themselves
and value this in others. In short, their managerial strengths lie

in: easily creating stability; understanding and conserving values and policies; straightforward common sense; being well planned, decisive, and reliable; running efficient meetings; and seeing things through.

In their dealings with colleagues they want them to come to the point and stick to the point, they are clearcut – people know where they stand with them. However, they tend to see and comment primarily on weaknesses, regarding the strengths as obvious and good performance as no more than is to be expected; they may withhold 'strokes' unless fully deserved, and feel more comfortable giving strokes symbolically (trophies, awards) rather than face to face transactions, and are not always accurate in their perception of interpersonal transactions. In addition, they have a tendency to recruit people in their own image rather than look for variety and diversity.

In the management team they concentrate their efforts on making the system run smoothly; are excellent at planning, execution, and operationalization, and keep those around them well informed of operational matters. They may be less skilled at managing the people system than either the economic or the technical system and may give too much of their attention to the satisfactory performer, seeing the poor performer as culpable and unworthy of help. However, their talent for engendering stability can go too far, leading to esteeming means above ends and being unable to look beyond the policies and rules to the principles underlying them; sometimes they even develop new procedures for the sole purpose of maintaining old procedures, and of all people they are the most likely to resist change.

Stress, for such people, comes from ambiguity. They prefer things to be clear: the data, the goals, and the plans for achieving them. When this is not so, they fret. Stress comes from having unclear objectives; in particular when the lack of clarity of objectives comes from (as they see it) people's whims and fancies. They dislike change, particularly when it is brought about by people whom they regard as having no respect for tradition, as not sharing their own standards, or not having 'served their time'. And because they become committed to their own plans, they dislike having to change their plans suddenly or having their diaries messed about. They become impatient when plans are delayed. Their *stress reactions* reflect their personality;

because they are naturally detail-conscious, one reaction to stress is obsessional checking and rechecking of the details, or going back and restating the objectives. Because they prefer structure and find it rewarding, they may react to stress by redoubling the structures and controls. All this has a tendency to slow down their own rate of work and the rate of work of people who depend on them. They may also seek to eliminate ambiguity when the situation is genuinely ambiguous, thus pursuing a goal which for them is clear but which also happens to be wrong. And they can react to failure of their efforts by deploying more resources, rather than by trying a different tack or admitting that it's an insoluble problem; if 10,000 soldiers don't do the trick you send in 50,000, or if the lady doesn't unbend for a dozen roses you send six dozen.

To summarize: the 'corporate concrete' problem comes about because the natural growth patterns of organizations in the Western world attracted, and for many years rewarded, a management style characterized by stabilizing, regulating, and reducing risk; such managers tend to be resistant to change and insecure in ambiguous situations. And they tend to recruit people in their own image.

Chapter 10 discusses transformational leadership. If you're the kind of person who starts to read books from the back, you'll already know something about transformational leaders. For a better understanding of the full nature of the corporate concrete problem, though, we need to compare the differences between the stabilizing manager and the transformational leader, because in those differences lie so many of the difficulties of getting the middle managers committed (see Table 5.1).

Bearing in mind the history of the corporate concrete problem, if we examine the interaction between the transformational manager and the stabilizing manager we stand rather more chance of being able to help the corporate concrete move towards the next stage – the organization of tomorrow.

Cracking through the corporate concrete

1   Acknowledge openly that it's because of their past contribution that the organization is strong enough to move on.

Table 5.1
Differences between the stabilizing manager and the transformational manager

	Stabilizing manager	Transformational manager
Orientation:	Past, tradition	Future
Thinking:	Linear, single-channel	Divergent, multi-channel
Communicate:	Likes to tie up all loose ends	May not bother to state what to him/her is obvious
Understanding:	Down-to-earth, demonstrable, provable	Metaphors, visions, broad brush
Planning:	Begin at the beginning and go on to the end, then stop	Needs only an intuitive grasp of the whole picture, need not state all the steps on the way
Persistence:	Prefers to finish things off, thorough	Likes to start new things, may get bored easily
Problem solving:	Prefers to apply past experience	Prefers to look for new ways
When things go wrong:	May redouble efforts in the teeth of the evidence	Likely to try a change of course
Hierarchy:	Respects and is at home in it	Disrespects and challenges it
Rewards:	Status, formal awards	Achievement
Attitude to regulations:	Useful, make things predictable, easier to manage	Stifling, to be challenged, unnecessary
Attitude to change:	Tends to resist it	Tends to welcome it
Risk-taking	Likes proof in advance	Takes a chance
Under stress:	Slows down, concentrates on managing the detail	Speeds up, becomes expedient

2   State as clearly as you can the reasons why the changes are necessary. Use models of organizational change and respected authorities. The changes should not appear to be fad or fashion.
3   It is not enough to paint a picture or share a vision of the end-point. Provide as clear a map as possible of the journey you will travel together, with timetables and progress checks.
4   Don't rely solely on metaphor to convey your message.
5   Use, value, and reward their ability to see a task through to completion.
6   Keep your promises.
7   If the situation is likely to remain ambiguous for some time, at least share your expectations of when things will become clearer.
8   Use your own status or seniority as Mountbatten used his – wearing his medals not because he needed to, but because the troops needed to see he'd earned them.
9   Aim to out-perform the rumour network at every turn.
10   Recognize and reward changes in performance, their own and the organization's, as quickly and visibly as you can.

Acknowledge openly that it's because of their past contribution that the organization is strong enough to move on

This happens to be true. Your organization may be choking on its own bureaucracy now, but there was a time – in most organizations a fairly long time – when these managers' stabilizing strengths were its salvation. If you don't believe me, look at the difficulties that small companies encounter when they start growing – what they need is systems and controls and procedures, and managers who are good at devising them. You're not saying that yesterday was bad (though it may have gone on too long!), just that tomorrow has to be different.

State as clearly as you can the reasons why the changes are necessary. Use models of organizational change and respected authorities. The changes should not appear to be fad or fashion

The transformational leader tends to scan the future naturally, welcomes change, and greets the unknown with energetic curiosity. For such a leader, therefore, the need for change is more likely to be obvious than for the stabilizing manager. To recruit the stabilizing manager's support, it's necessary to spell out the reasons for change, and to recruit as much hard evidence and authoritative support as you can.

It is not enough to paint a picture or share a vision of the end-point. Provide as clear a map as possible of the journey you will travel together, with timetables and progress checks

These two points can be taken together. The stabilizing managers' strengths lie in their ability to initiate procedures and see them through. The transformational leader is often content to draw a picture of the future as s/he sees it and assume that people will be able to translate this into action; for the corporate concrete this is a source of ambiguity and pain. Just to share with people the model of organization change I give in the Appendix, for example (p.144), will show them that the path of transformation is not uncertain, nor is it being embarked upon because somebody's read the latest management book. They need to know (*a*) that the journey is inevitable, (*b*) that there is a map, and (*c*) that it's possible to use the map to tell how well they're doing.

Don't rely solely on metaphor to convey your message

Two reasons for this one. First, because while we have to use metaphor to picture the kind of transformed organization, and transformed people, that we want to be, if we then stay at the level of metaphor we will not have done the necessary task of operationalizing the metaphor – run it through the video test of *'What we are going to be able to observe people doing differently?'* The second reason is that you need to engage the stabilizing managers' abilities to make things happen; when an organizational transformation is going well, it's the stabilizing managers, who may have been the corporate concrete until they got a new lease of life, who can take the visions of the transformational leaders, sort the wheat from the chaff and the workable from the unworkable, and see them through to completion. Make the bridge between the vision and what we're going to do on Tuesday.

Use, value, and reward their ability to see a task through to completion

I treasure one lovely example of this, a partnership between a research director and his second-in-command. The director had many of the characteristics of the transformational leader; his deputy was more of a stabilizer. The director said of his deputy: 'He's the one who takes my mad ideas and tells me which ones will work. He's the one who takes them from a drawing on blotting paper to the factory floor. He's the one who prevents me from re-inventing the wheel, because he's got such a store of experience to draw on.' And the deputy of the director: 'He does the mad scientist bit, and that's fine by me. What *I* like is drawing up the plans for getting the show on the road; looking round the factory floor, months after he's moved on to something new, and thinking *"Without me, this would still be all in the air"*.' The corporate concrete made their contribution by seeing things through; maybe in the past few years they've been seeing through the wrong things, but once that practical ability is reoriented . . ..

Keep your promises

A leader who breaks promises is painful to anyone, whatever their psychological make up. The stabilizing manager's natural respect for authority, though, is likely to mean that a broken promise by the leader is seen as a broken promise by the whole organization, and to linger as remembered pain long after other people might have forgotten it.

If the situation is likely to remain ambiguous for some time, at least share your expectations of when things will become clearer

Both these points address the stabilizing managers' dislike of ambiguity, and their need to feel that the organization repays the loyalty they have given it. Of course, not every promise can be kept, there are factors outside every manager's control. And not every transformational journey can be programmed into a daily timetable. If you put yourself in the shoes of a manager who reached his/her position by helping the organization make life more predictable and controllable, then you may understand how insecure they feel when asked to surrender their old ways of doing things without any sense of certainty.

Use your own status or seniority as Mountbatten used his – wearing his medals not because he needed to, but because the troops needed to see he'd earned them

Engage the corporate concrete's capacity for loyalty to the organization and its leaders; show them that they are working for someone who's come under fire but can still display the human touch; but don't go into battles based purely on status, because a recalcitrant chunk of corporate concrete probably knows more about winning these than any transformational leader does.

Aim to out-perform the rumour network at every turn

When change is in the air, the rumour network flourishes. Try to achieve a situation where the best, most up-to-date, and most accurate information about the organization comes from its leaders, wherever they be in the hierarchy. Use briefing groups, videos, newsletters, personal chats (lots of these) to get the information across. In particular, aim to out-perform the trade union rumour network. If you can fix a fax on every noticeboard with the results of the latest union meeting before the shop stewards have spread their own version, you're winning. (Unions have their own corporate concrete too, and less pressure to change.)

Recognize and reward changes in performance, their own and the organization's, as quickly and visibly as you can

I don't mean through the merit payment system, nor the annual sales convention in exotic places. I mean personal congratulations, celebrations, parties, personal notes. Albert Koopman, the Cashbuild story referred to in Chapter 3, had himself converted into an Albert the Lion figure, and had a library of cartoon memoranda he used to send people after his visits: a beaming

Albert the Lion saying 'Well done' for special customer service (and here's an 'Extra Mile' cheque), a happy Albert saying that he'd just seen morale at its best, a contented Albert distributing money because he'd seen an example of good stock management. (And, of course, various 'Albert the Lion is displeased' memoranda: you've slipped badly, you're turning a deaf ear, pick up the pieces and fix.) It doesn't work if people haven't the foggiest idea who Albert the Lion is, so you'd better be the kind of visible leader whose opinion they value. Of course, the meta-message behind the use of personal congratulations is that people see their leader as noticing and caring about what's going on.

Almost the end of the chapter on corporate concrete. We began with a description of them as middle managers, typically resistant to change, needing to be worked on, maybe even fired, because they wouldn't go along with the new ways of doing things. Gentle reader, are you by any chance now tired of the phrase, and the assumptions behind it? If you are, then jolly good. The corporate concrete behaviour is a function of what's been rewarded in the past; selective recruitment and training; and our common inability to come to terms with the fact that from time to time there are qualitative shifts in the way societies and organizations need to manage themselves. Maybe the only thing history teaches us is that people do not learn from history.

> If you have nothing better to do one day, take a tumbler and fill it full of fleas. The fleas will jump out of the tumbler. So you keep them contained by putting a piece of paper over the top of the tumbler. Sooner or later the fleas will tire of hitting their little heads on the paper, and learn to jump less high.
>
> When you later take the paper away, how high do you think the fleas will jump?

6 Empires, empowerment and entrepreneurs

In the disabling – or disabled – organization, you often hear two cries of protest: 'That's not my job!' and 'Keep off, that's my job!' It's called empire building, and it gets in the way.

Like corporate concrete, empire building is the result of something once useful but now carried too far. When the organization was growing from small to medium-sized, the introduction of specialist functions and the split into line and staff functions, head office and branches or divisions, was necessary; it allowed people to concentrate on their own field. The manufacturing manager could carry on manufacturing, knowing that there was a marketing function to take care of selling his efforts, a finance function to pay for the materials used, and a personnel function to ensure that the staff were fairly treated.

But, carried too far, specialist functions result in a situation where almost anything a manager wants to do is thwarted because there's a department claiming it as their province, or a requirement for head office to sign-off. In many organizations, too, this trend led to the favouring of the specialist departments over the producing departments: you could see this in people's career paths, for instance. Join the manufacturing department as, say, a graduate trainee, and you would probably be faced with several years of hard slog before you reached any seniority; your peers who had joined personnel, or finance, or the legal department would long ago have outstripped you. There's also the legacy of the days of galloping inflation and stock market deregulation, when the finance manager could make more money overnight by nifty trading than the sales or production side could with weeks of sweat. Add to that the fact that the average bean-counter could (often still can) spend their days saying 'Here's where you went wrong' and 'No, you can't do that', while the average production manager spends his or her days doing things (and, inevitably, doing some of them in a way that the bean-counters disapprove of) and you have a neat recipe for the decline of manufacturing industry as a whole. It's become a game with lots of referees and no players.

> He that hath much to do will do something wrong, and of that wrong must suffer the consequences; and if it were possible that he should always act rightly, yet when such numbers are to judge of his conduct, the bad will censure and obstruct him by malevolence, and the good sometimes by mistake.
>
> Samuel Johnson, *Rasselas*

Hence the title of this chapter: the three E's – Empires (the breaking thereof); Empowerment (the doing thereof); and Entrepreneurs (the encouragement thereof). Let's start with empire building: how can we engineer its decline and fall?

Empire building – its decline and fall

1   Head office changes its role from a custodian of the word 'No' to an internal consultancy and tame merchant bank.
2   Day-to-day responsibility for specialist functions is returned as far as possible into the hands of line managers.
3   Specialists regard themselves as providing a service to line managers, who are their customers.
4   Producing departments are given parity of esteem, at least, with advisory departments.
5   The finance function, in particular, changes its role from archaeology to exploration.
6   Long-term career planning ensures that every employee has experience of working for a variety of functions, especially customer service.

Head office changes its role from a custodian of the word 'No' to an internal consultancy and tame merchant bank

In other words, head office sees its role as enabler, sponsor – whatever word will reflect the new way of doing things – which is to help line managers make things happen. Head office becomes the place where managers go for advice; for resources; for help with networking; for consultation on matters where a general precedent may be set. There are still many functions for head office to carry out, because they are best handled centrally; largely, these are the representative functions, where one head office has to speak to another head office (e.g. that of a national or international customer, supplier, trade union) as the voice of the organization. There are plenty of things for the general to do, but looking over the captains' shoulders is no longer one of them.

Day-to-day responsibility for specialist functions is returned, as far as possible, into the hands of line managers

The current concern for making quality everyone's responsibility is a good example of this. In the bad old days, when there was a quality assurance department, it was easy to slip into the habit of thinking 'We'll do the minimum to get by, and our mistakes will be rectified by the QA department, or the retailers, or the dealers. . .'. In the worst cases, and there were many of them, the quality control was done by the poor customers, by seeing what they complained most vociferously about; or by consumer magazines and television programmes.

Quality is not the only function that could and should be handed back to the line. Many personnel decisions, purchasing decisions, decisions about maintenance, advertising, merchandizing . . . the question is not 'What could we easily part with?' but 'What must we absolutely hang on to at head office?' So this strategy will only work in conjunction with the first point – head office must change its role to adviser, sponsor, resourcer – and be seen by the rest of the organization to be a better adviser and resourcer than any available elsewhere.

Specialists regard themselves as providing a service to line managers, who are their customers

This point is obvious in the light of the first two. But how do you achieve it? A simple and obvious place to start is to ask whether the specialists have ever met their internal customers on their own ground. It's quite possible they haven't. I once worked for a large multinational manufacturing company which wanted to assess the capabilities of young managers to run operations in Africa. This was typically a young person's job: graduate trainees would be eligible after a few years working in head office. Not all the assignments had been successful; given the high cost of failure they wanted to be clearer about what they should look for in a good man in Africa.

We conducted some research with a sample of managers from the UK head office and from Africa, to discover what the phrase 'effective management' meant to them. Clear differences showed in the two groups' prescriptions for effectiveness.

Head office managers concentrated heavily on planning and analysis skills; rational decision making; careful preparation of cases, including written communication skills. By contrast, the Africa-based managers concentrated on stamina and stress management; the ability to think on one's feet and cope without a formal support system; informal, largely oral, communications skills; leadership ability and industrial relations skills. As one manager put it: 'In head office they steam up when they don't get an instant response to our telex, and here in the field we may only get electricity for four hours a day'.

That's an extreme example, but I know of many organizations where the specialists never go on visits to the line; where they cook up wonderful ideas which have no chance of working in practice. I also know many other organizations where the early stages of the transformation process involve a letter from the new MD asking each specialist function to cost-justify itself, not merely in terms of costs, but also in terms of service. It goes hard, that.

Producing departments are given parity of esteem, at least, with advisory departments

This is one initiative that can only be managed from head office. And getting it to pass the video test – (What could we capture on film to show that production departments now have parity of esteem?) – is not easy. What are you doing to make sure that your best graduate recruits are attracted into the production departments? And have commensurate salary expectations? When you do your equal opportunities review, are you considering how many minorities there are on the operations side as well as the clerical side? What are you doing to ensure that the advisory departments have to make a case to the production departments rather than the other way around?

The finance function, in particular, changes its role from archaeology to exploration

Once when I was interviewing the finance director of an organization in the middle of a transformation, I said to him: 'You're not like any other finance director I've met. Why?' 'Ah,' he said, 'I want to create a new profession. The accountant as catalyst.' And then he outlined to me his plans to go from eighty accountants based at head office to twenty-five, of whom eight would be in head office and the rest attached to line managers, as part of the field management teams, where they would be expected to take decisions as well as report on their consequences. He was quite amusing about the way some of them had responded when charged with the responsibility of getting the company's mud on their boots.

Long-term career planning ensures that every employee has experience of working for a variety of functions, especially customer service

I remember running a management assessment programme looking for board-level potential. One of the participants was a scientist, a truly lovely man. He was a brilliant R&D director; a mouth-watering profile on the psychological test battery; strong leadership characteristics. The one thing that stood in his way was that he had never acquired any financial management experience, and very little marketing experience. In his early 50s, it was too late to suggest that he quit being a scientist for a bit to gain this experience; and so, although there were two overseas general management posts which he could, in principle, have eaten for breakfast, he had to be turned down in favour of people less good but with wider experience. That was nearly ten years ago, and he's probably retired to grow roses; for me, it's a remembered pain as clear as yesterday. I wanted to reach back into his past and alter a couple of knobs on the control panel.

His is not an unusual case, of course. And as organizations move towards cutting out layers, cases like his become more important. At a strategic level they can only be handled by head office career planning; it's an unusual specialist who will voluntarily take him or herself out of their specialist career path for a year, losing parity with their peers, while they gain experience in another department. Company-wide, though, this leads to stove-pipe management: where everyone climbs up the narrow little stove-pipes of their own speciality, to emerge several years later peering fearfully over the top to look at their competitors. We can't afford such limitations.

> When Chris Green took over as general manager of ScotRail, his first act was to take an hour's phone-in on Radio Clyde, talking with people who wanted to know what to expect of the railway in Scotland. (How he did it I don't know, because he and I had polished off a bottle of 1972 Hermitage the night before.) He came back with his pockets stuffed full of names and phone numbers of all the people who had tried and failed to get through; these were evenly distributed throughout all his senior officers (including engineering and finance and personnel and all the folk who never saw a customer) with the instructions to phone them up, find out what they wanted, answer them if possible, and report back to him by lunch-time.

Empowerment

The second E stands for empowerment. It sounds good, and in many organizations it's a vogue word. It is also more difficult, and more rewarding, than most people think. It is not just a matter of redrawing the lines on the organization chart and issuing everyone with new job descriptions. It takes real, prolonged effort. Too often I've heard comments like 'They're supposed to have been empowered, why don't they do something?' and 'We've told the branch managers they have freedom to behave in a more commercial fashion, but it doesn't seem to have made any difference'. The hard answer is that maybe they haven't done enough.

Empowerment is a change in the contract between two parties. One party is the group of junior managers who, so the theory goes, have been frustrated until now by the head office bureaucracy. They are by definition closer to the customer; they are the ones who see new things for the organization to do, opportunities they cannot act on because it is difficult to energize head office. They are the ones who have their local priorities dowsed by the head office bargaining processes, who have to implement systems that don't quite fit their needs because head office has a spurious concern for uniformity. They are the ones who have to manage by a rule book they never made, are prevented from taking risks, and after a while often see their main task as the production of defensive paperwork.

So far so good. But what about the other party to the contract, head office? If junior line managers are to be given more power and authority, then head office must learn to relinquish some power and authority of its own. Without that renunciation, the line managers will feel, rightly, that they have been bamboozled. At worst, you'll have another expensive demonstration of Stewart's Law of Reorganization: that structural solutions to functional problems don't work.

Here therefore, is a ten-point checklist relating to head office's part in the empowerment contract. Some of the points relate to head office systems and controls; others, more difficult and more important, relate to issues of hearts and minds, to commitment and personal example.

Have you really empowered your managers?

1   Are you responding more quickly to ideas and suggestions?
2   Are you really rewarding good ideas?
3   Have you delegated authority, or just delegated work?
4   Have managers the freedom not to rely on head office at all?
5   Are you seeking uniformity and conformity for its own sake?
6   Do you issue rules, or do you discuss principles?
7   Systems can be a frame or a cage.
8   If the system is to be broken, where is the burden of proof?
9   Diluting local priorities means diluting local authority.
10   Is the customer's voice heard?

Are you responding more quickly to ideas and suggestions?

I was recently told the story of one particular organizational transformation to the top managers of a big Australasian insurance company, whose top managers claimed to have empowered its branch managers to behave like entrepreneurs. I related the story of how local managers, previously hampered by a spending limit of £25, had been given the freedom to spend seven tranches of £10,000 without reference to head office – provided that they spent it on visible improvements to staff care or customer care – and the freedom to put up proposals for investing larger sums. What made my audience prick up their ears was the tale of one area which put up a proposal for spending £197,000 and had a 'Yes' answer from the new general manager within three days. The story illustrated the energizing effect on the area managers of that quick response – the delight, and the responsibility, in finding that the general manager demanded a yesable proposition and knew what to do with it. The story had an additional effect on my audience however; one of them summed it up afterwards thus: 'We thought we had done the job when we told line managers to assemble groups to put up suggestions. But you've made us realize that their suggestions have to go through the same old head office grinding mill. By the time we've responded, they'll think we've forgotten about them.' They were right in their perceptions. If head office requests suggestions and proposals, but then sits on them, the meta-message is that the commercial urgency which gave rise to the notion of empowerment is not shared by head office.

Are you really rewarding good ideas?

In other words, what have you done to energize the gossip network so that every instance of empowered behaviour receives favourable publicity? You have to counteract the previous years of people feeling that 'I can't even suggest it because I know they won't allow it'. Remember, it's not the size of the reward that counts half so much as the speed of the reward and the message it conveys that the act, or the good idea, has been noticed. At British Rail, we introduced a system of Service Excellence vouchers. They were carried by certain senior managers who, if they saw an instance of outstanding customer service, could go up to the person concerned and say: 'I saw that. It was great (and here's why). Here's a voucher for £10, which you can cash in at the end of your shift, and the certificate will be in the post'. Can you imagine the effect? Not just the 'Gee, they saw me doing that . . . they're not walking around with their noses in the air after all,' but the effect on the person's pride as s/he was able to walk into the office at the end of the shift and have co-workers see him or her collecting the reward.

Have you delegated authority, or just delegated work?

I described earlier an exercise which people are asked to play when we're working on organizational transformation: senior managers must be explicit, using the video test, about what they want empowered subordinates to do differently. It's uncomfortable, because it raises the contrast between delegating work and delegating authority. An empowered manager is not one who has more work on his or her plate; empowered managers have *different* tasks, tasks they can and do initiate themselves, tasks that previously they would have had to ask permission to engage in.

Have managers the freedom not to rely on head office at all?

'I wanted to buy a calculator. It cost four times my limit of authority, even though I'm a senior design engineer. I can't just go out and buy it; I have to ask central purchasing. They are under an edict to see whether they can obtain it wholesale; so, instead of buying one for me, they design a form on which anyone can say whether they want a calculator, and they send it out to every engineer of my level and above. Of course, the others don't want one, so the form is low priority and sits at the bottom of their in-tray. And my four-figure calculator is pretty low priority for central purchasing, given the multimillion deals they'd prefer to spend their time on, so they don't chase it either; and I don't know who is dealing with it in central purchasing so it's difficult for me to chase. To cut a long story short, it would be eight months before I got it through the system, so I do what everyone else does – invent four purchases within my limit of authority, and nip round the corner and buy it. Oh, by the way, it doesn't half make it difficult for me to deal with petty fiddling by my own staff when they see me fiddling my own expenses!'

In a disabling organization so many things fall victim to this spirit; managers do not have the authority to do the small things quickly. They have to rely on head office functions. The freedom to make minor purchases; to use a local plumber rather than call on central maintenance; to buy uniform shirts from Marks and Spencer if the central stores run out – these freedoms are a necessary part of empowerment. And, by the way, it's amazing what the head office functions find themselves capable of, if they sense that their protected empires may face competition.

Are you seeking uniformity and conformity for its own sake?

Rules, systems, and procedures devised centrally are rarely a perfect fit when they come to be applied locally. The empowered manager has the freedom to challenge that uniformity; the disempowered manager lacks it. Personnel systems are particularly prone to spurious uniformity; for example, the performance appraisal system judges a research engineer and a sales manager on the same criteria because head office finds it convenient to use the same forms for everybody. Then there's the department store manager who cannot get through to head office the fact that she would like more size 16 dresses and fewer size 8's – head office has a system for allocating different sizes, and it's not negotiable; British Rail used to calculate the number of staff selling tickets according to total revenue, ignoring the fact that commuter stations sell a high volume of cheaper tickets. If the custodians of the systems regard their job as servicing their managers, their first concern will be that line managers have the information, and the authority, that they need to do the job; if this results in a certain lack of uniformity, the reconciliation takes place in head office.

Do you issue rules, or do you discuss principles?

Rule-dependent organizations are disabling organizations. I make no apology for repeating this point.

> Have you ever heard Bob Newhart's sketch about the janitor in the Empire State Building when it was attacked by King Kong? 'I looked

it up under Ape, and Ape's Toes, but I couldn't find anything in the instruction book . . . I took a broom out of the store-cupboard even though I didn't have a requisition note . . . my authority only extends to the seventeenth floor . . .'

Systems can be a frame or a cage

Organizations which have genuinely empowered their managers move from having controlling systems to enabling systems. A controlling system is one which imposes a ceiling on people above which they cannot rise; an enabling system is one which gives them a floor below which they have no excuse for falling. A controlling system collects data on absolutely everything within its purview; an enabling system checks only what it needs to check, and from time to time takes a micrometer slice through the organization to see if there are any sub-critical problems that need acting upon. A controlling system is oriented towards finding faults; an enabling system, towards opportunities. Chapter 8 is all about developing enabling systems.

If the system is to be broken, where is the burden of proof?

When NASA's head office scheduled its shuttle flights, it planned a launch in February 1985. When the date came, engineers on the ground became aware of certain danger signs associated with component failures at low temperatures. (Not just engineers, by the way. One of the early warnings came from an accountant, who'd been looking at some figures and working out some correlations.) They sent an urgent message to head office about their fears, asking to postpone the launch. Head office replied: 'What do you want to do, postpone the programme till April? We've got a schedule to meet.' Most of us saw the explosive, tragic results on our television screens.

These professionals were not empowered to act on their data and intuitions. They had to prove to head office – a head office with different priorities, priorities to do with satisfying its political paymasters – that they wanted to bust the system. When managers are truly empowered, the burden of proof should be on head office to tell them why they can't, rather than on them to prove why they should.

Diluting local priorities means diluting local authority

A branch manager has a problem with an unsatisfactory employee. She calls in the employee and starts the disciplinary procedure. The employee then calls in the nationally-organized union, and the problem moves from the branch to head office. There, the personnel director is working for union acceptance of a work restructuring scheme. In a disabling organization, the problem of disciplining one employee becomes a low priority for the personnel director when compared with the other issues on his plate. Therefore, it may not be treated quickly; it may not be treated at all; at worst, it is eagerly welcomed by the personnel director as a heaven-sent opportunity to make a small concession in return for acceptance of his pet scheme.

Back at the branch, one manager has the feeling that her own head office has undermined her authority. Eventually she will come to tolerate poor performers because she knows that trying to do something about them will bring her trouble on two fronts.

Within an organization, on a global scale, you can draw a hierarchy of priorities as seen from head office; and sometimes it is necessary for a local manager's wishes to give way to a greater organizational need. But when managers are empowered, the head office realizes that there are certain priorities which are absolute for the people concerned, even though they may be small when compared with the larger issues. When head office dilutes these priorities it must be aware that it also dilutes the manager's authority, and takes away the manager's power.

Is the customer's voice heard?

Empowerment is difficult: it demands more tolerance of ambiguity and uncertainty. The certainty of rules and procedures is replaced by moves towards principles, initiatives, variety, and the occasional mistake. So there must be some touchstones, some key values against which the changes are to be measured. One indispensable principle is that of customer service. Disempowered managers are often frustrated because they cannot give their customers satisfaction; when they are empowered, they can respond to the voice of the customer. The criterion of increased customer satisfaction should be a difficult one to evade.

Entrepreneurs

The third and final E in this chapter is entrepreneur. The transformed organization is one in which people feel that their natural inventiveness, or sense of 'there must be a better way to do this', stands a good chance of being heard. The *Cosmopolitan* story in Chapter 2 is an excellent example – a leader determined to create such a climate.

Recently the word 'intrapreneur' came into use. I didn't like it, partly because I have a pedant's dislike of neologisms, but more importantly because its use implied that people had forgotten what the word 'entrepreneur' originally meant. The term was coined by the economist J.B. Say, and its definition is simple and beautiful:

> An entrepreneur is one who moves resources from areas of low productivity to areas of high productivity.

And there you have it. All you need to be an entrepreneur is a hunger for cost-effectiveness, a natural dislike of waste, and constant vigilance for opportunities to kill two birds with one stone. (I had a Czech friend who used to translate that as 'killing two chickens with one brick'.) You don't have to be a small business, or a one-man band. You can be an entrepreneur anywhere you like.

However, many of the attempts to promote intrapreneuring (the last time but one I shall use the word) failed. You don't hear the word used much nowadays. Reasons?

It has to be part of a '*gestalt*' – a vision in which the whole is greater than the sum of its parts. There have been many pocket solutions – quality circles, customer care programmes etc. which organizations have used like sticking plaster, instead of listening to the message behind the solution. If you chip away the bottom left-hand bit of the marble block, you can't kid yourself it's David; it's a marble block with a left foot looking rather foolish at the bottom, and if the imprisoned David had any feelings he'd be embarrassed and trying very hard to pull his foot back in. When the adopted solution is not part of a '*gestalt*', not only does it fail on its own terms, it conveys to everyone else in the organization that its leaders think they can solve problems by learning a few new words and throwing some money around.

Nearly all attempts to formalize the process fail, because you're trying to formalize spontaneity. It's like making an appointment to make love. There are some organizations with a well-developed system for supporting entrepreneurs. I remember the manager of one, who described how ideas could be put up through his immediate manager, and the next manager up, and then there was an independent appeals system to a person with a discretionary budget. What struck me most, when I listened to him, was not so much the system he described as the humour with which he described it; he was mockingly aware of the organization's own bureaucracy and the means it had had to adopt to prevent it stifling innovation.

Yet another reason is scale. People who were caught up with the fashion for intrapreneuring often, I believe, thought that they would soon be deluged with new ideas for back-yard nuclear power stations, chicken-powered supersonic flight, and palatable cures for baldness and lost virility. In fact, what they – you – should be seeking to encourage is the small improvements: cutting out a form here, a procedure there, a component elsewhere. Paradoxically, it's only in climates where people feel free to improve the small things that the big ones have freedom to emerge.

Final reason for failure: most inventions happen by happy accident, and *most inventors have fun*. This is hardly mentioned in the literature on in-house entrepreneuring. I remember reading, in my youth, Robert Jungk's account of turn-of-the-century nuclear physics; he described the atmosphere in Göttingen, where some of the best work was done: the café proprietors under instruction not to wash tablecloths if they had formulae on them, professors riding out on their bikes at 0430 to tell students about bright ideas they'd just had . . . the whole picture was one of buzz, fun, discovery, mutual respect and mutual forgiveness, celebration – above all, excitement. Somehow that atmosphere didn't figure in the solemn books on intrapreneuring. But we're not very good at thinking about work and fun in the same breath, are we?

So if you want to build an organization which supports people's entrepreneurial abilities, my advice is – don't try. Trying will kill it. Concentrate on removing the obstacles, the bureaucracy, the paralysis by analysis, the corporate concrete: and on building the leadership, teamwork, and commitment which figure in the second part of this book. Then, when David walks out of his marble block, he'll be saying 'Have I got an idea for you!'

Interlude

Before I move on to the second half of this book, may I beg
a moment's thought for those people who, when they thought
about the marble blocks that barred them from achieving their full
potential, labelled the blocks with words like 'racism', 'disability',
'gender', 'religious intolerance', and 'the pain of leaving one's
community to look for work elsewhere?' These are not blocks
which every David can break out of single-handedly; though, as
I write, Stephen Hawking's *A Brief History of Time* is still on
the best-seller list and showing, so beautifully, what a mind can
do even when the body is useless.

I wish I had something constructive to say to such people,
something that wouldn't sound patronizing, or be yet another
version of the 'society must change' platitudes. I've lived in a
number of divided societies, working directly on the issues that
divide them – Northern Ireland, South Africa, New Zealand, and
the American Indians. I have one perception to share from this
experience, and two stories.

I believe that there is more chance of healing such divisions if,
somehow, the out-group can find things to give to the in-group,
rather than just learning to accept their way. In New Zealand, for
example, I am struck by how the Maori people are giving aspects
of their culture to the basically Western organizational structure;
lending their sense of time-perspective, of a holistic approach, of
the place of music and laughter and common relaxation, to people

driven by a different set of values. I've seen European managers go to their first meeting on a marae (Maori ceremonial meeting-place) full of fear and trembling, and return touched, moved – and no less able to take good business decisions. It's by no means a perfect example of two cultures living together (and there are more than two – Auckland has the biggest population of Pacific Islanders in the Pacific basin), and it might yet erupt into trouble, but there is a sense of the whole becoming greater than the sum of its parts.

I was so moved by some of the initiatives I saw there that my mouth started watering at what might be possible if the message could be taken to South Africa. I said as much to Waereti Tait-Rolleston, one of the leading Maori women, who's been charged by her tribe with helping to build cross-cultural bridges. Here's what she said:

> Some of our elders went on a visit there, and came back grieved. Yet we agreed that we might have something to offer them. The elders held a long hui and came to the conclusion that, first, we must be more certain than we are that we are making good progress here.
>
> Then we fell to talking about who our message should go to. Should we try to meet with the black leaders, and if so, who? And our chief reached for a loaf of bread, and held it in front of him. 'When you give someone a loaf,' he said, 'you do not slice it for them first, nor tell them how they should divide it. If, and when, we have something to give to South Africa, it will be a gift to everyone there, whatever their colour or religion.'

And the second story, which for me says how it should be:

> Chris Green, then General manager of ScotRail, called together some people to form an equal opportunities group. (Incidentally, it met for the first time on the morning that the results of a guards' strike ballot were to be announced; never once did he leave the room, or receive progress messages, which gave me another example of the leader trusting his staff enough to put his energies into making the future better.) 'I'm not doing this because it's fashionable, or legally required, or because the board says so,' he said. 'I'm doing it because I'm tired of not having access to the skills and abilities of half the workforce, and it's up to you to see that I get it.'

This interlude is not a soft-hearted moralistic plea: it's saying that as long as we imprison other people in the blocks of our own prejudice we impoverish ourselves at least as much as we impoverish them.

7 Customers first

Somewhere in my disorganized archives I have a report that I'm proud of, because of the date and because of what it led to. It's a report to the general manager of the Eastern Region of British Rail, dated 1981, and it says that we've lost touch with our customers and we have to start listening to them and trying to give them what they want. The insight that I'm particularly proud of, and which was the toughest to get accepted, was that the most difficult and most important task would not be training our customer contact staff, but would lie in persuading all managers, particularly the ones who'd never cast eyes on a customer, to accept the customer first initiatives.

Once we started work, we discovered a number of endemic problems which, I suspect, occur to a greater or lesser extent in all big bureaucratic organizations that have lost sight of their customers.

The selection criteria for customer contact staff were still based in the days when the job was largely clerical. Employees were recruited on the basis of their ability with figures, not their ability to relate to people. Even the simplest of modern technology makes the clerical aspects of the work less important compared with the human relations aspects, but we hadn't seen that.

We didn't see our sales outlets as sales outlets. Places like booking offices and travel centres were seen as a cost to be borne (by the operating side, furthermore) rather than as a shop window. This was reflected not only in simple things like the standard of decoration and general ease of finding one's way around the place, but also by the fact that the operating side, which is largely concerned with the day-to-day running of trains, saw the booking offices and travel centres as the first place to take the strain when there was a freeze on recruitment, for example.

Even worse was the way we treated the telephone enquiry bureaux. Besides being run on inadequate and out-of-date equipment, they were largely staffed by three kinds of people: those who had withdrawn from face-to-face contact with the public of their own free will, those who had been put there for disciplinary reasons and, probably worst of all, new starters in the booking office travel centre grades, who had been put to work on the telephones on the extraordinary assumption that this was an easier job than answering queries face-to-face.

Hidden in the previous example is the fact that we would demote staff into positions of customer contact. Too often the mournful chap on the wrong end of a yard brush or clipping tickets on the platform, or serving in the booking office, would be there because of a demotion for disciplinary reasons; in other words, employees who couldn't be trusted with the company's equipment or resources were asked to present the company's face to the customers.

Literature that should properly have been regarded as sales aids was seen as a drain on resources and therefore scarce. The timetable, for example, was published twice yearly and was sold out within a few days; some booking offices complained that they were unobtainable. Again, part of the problem was that timetable printing was the responsibility of the operating side, and therefore seen as a cost not a marketing investment.

We didn't train staff in customer contact skills. There were some jobs, like those of the guards, that had been changing steadily from primarily operating to primarily customer contact, but we gave them no help by way of training or coaching. When we did start training, we discovered that these unwitting ambassadors fell clearly into two groups – those who loved the customer contact role, and those who hated it and avoided it at every turn.

Managers above a certain level were allowed free first-class travel between home and place of work. On crowded services they were expected to give up their seats to fare-paying customers.

When the protests from customers that this was not happening reached intolerable proportions we issued reminders to managers. Resolutely many of them clung to their seats. Eventually the only way to deal with the problem was to withdraw the privilege completely.

Managers were insulated in many ways from the service their customers experienced. Most of them knew their way around the system well enough not to get lost, or to be able to guess the cause of any delay. They had travel vouchers which meant that they never had to queue for tickets. If managers with their identifying passes were travelling on trains, the guards would often seek them out to explain the reasons for a delay. And, if they were going to an important meeting and the train ground to a quiet halt somewhere picturesque, they knew that if the people they were meeting needed to know what had happened to them, all they had to do was to ring Control and they'd be told.

We judged the quality of the service on inadequate criteria. We tended to make judgements on the basis of the on-train experience only – was the train comfortable, fast, on time? All of which is important, but left out the beginning of the journey: car parking, buying the ticket, facilities on the station itself; and the end: getting through the ticket barrier, managing the luggage, finding the buses and taxis and telephones.

And so on. One of the problems the railway has to put up with is that everyone thinks they can run it better. Whatever country you're in, people remember their Hornby train sets and think that it must be like that but bigger. The problems we found on the railway are exactly the same as the problems in bringing customer care to an airline, a government department, a retail store, a manufacturing company, a health service or a school.

Here's a checklist for examining the degree to which you really put customers first in your organization.

Do we really put customers first?

1   Do the selection criteria for customer contact staff (all of them, not just the ones you might think of as customer contact staff) reflect the importance of customer contact to the job?
2   Do we see as sales opportunities all the occasions, places, and pieces of literature which we publish to our customers?

3   Do we demote people to positions of customer contact?
4   Do we train everyone who comes into contact with customers in customer contact skills, and with the knowledge necessary for them to help customers if required?
5   Do we ensure that all managers regularly experience the same service as the customers? And encourage them to take appropriate action if they see the service failing in any way?
6   Is there an expectation amongst the staff (or, worse, the customers) that if a senior manager's around they will pull their socks up and give better service?
7   Have we looked at the complete service your customers experience – from how they first enter into an association with us to when they leave it – and evaluated our service on that basis?
8   Do we have trouble calling them 'customers' in the first place?

There are probably more people in your organization with customer contact responsibility than you think. Even organizations which pride themselves on funnelling customers so that they have contact with only a limited number of trained people – retail stores, airlines and holiday companies, hotels – find that some customers will nonetheless meet the security staff, the baggage handlers, and the cooks. Some of them might want to ring head office with a query. Some may find themselves in prolonged negotiations with the accounts department. Everyone in the organization must understand that the customer pays their wages; and selecting and training with customer contact skills should be a higher priority criterion than at present.

The difficulty in obtaining a railway timetable is an extreme case – not many organizations make it as difficult to find out about their products as the railway used to. But there are plenty of other examples of organizational literature that put the customers off; I still can't understand the manual for my security system, or my oven, and the word-processor previous to this one had a manual which began with the electronic equivalent of '*Open the box with the crowbar you will find inside*'. (Not helped by the saleswoman who made it clear, *after* the sale, that if she spent more than twenty minutes explaining how to use it she had lost money on the sale.)

The insulation from the real quality of the product or service that managers, and specialists, often feel, is a danger. In some organizations this is relatively easy to remedy: they are encouraged to sample the service, take the products home and use them, or go out and sell them. Others are more difficult. You can't break a leg to test the quality of the health care you offer. But you can carry out a test – and, please, at unusual times, and without prior notice. When, as sometimes happens, the staff feel obliged to put on a better performance because management's about, you'll never find out what life is like for the ordinary punter. I once had an assignment for a British motor manufacturer. Because of a company edict that foreign cars were not allowed on their premises, the Audi had to be left behind and I was picked up every morning by one of the senior managers. He had a brand-new model car, and every morning something was wrong with it – the windows didn't work, knobs had fallen off, the petrol cap wouldn't fit. He didn't understand it, because he'd been down to the line and earmarked that one for his own while it was still in embryo. For him the problem extended as far as getting the car looked at by the workshops while he was at work; after all, the company had an explicit policy of manufacturing 30,000 cars on a 'see what we can get away with' basis, after which it analysed the more glaring faults and put them right on the next run. I don't think he has a job any more, and I wonder if he's capable of making the connection between his own lack of response to poor product quality and the long-term viability of his industry.

Almost certainly, the customers' perceptions of your organization will be formed on a wider data-base than you think. When we focused on the train at the expense of the total journey, we missed important things. Something as simple as a post-sale phone call (not, definitely not, the same thing as a form letter congratulating you on having become the proud owner of a new microwave oven) makes the customer believe you really care, and will probably tell you things you need to know. Look, particularly, at whether the customers have *left* you when you think they have; often they haven't. Perceptions of an airline are influenced by the speed at which the baggage turns up (and how they treat the customer with lost baggage) and the terminal facilities; perceptions of a supermarket by the struggle with the trolley to the car; perceptions of an electrical product by the cry of despair when the customer remembers that in the UK it's rare for an appliance to come with a plug ready fitted.

Final point: maybe you don't relate to this because you don't think your organization has customers. Maybe you like to speak of them as clients, or patients, or pupils. Or as taxpayers, or subscribers, or beneficiaries. If so, the news is bad. First because the trend worldwide is for deregulation, privatization, and the destruction of monopolies; your nice comfortable monopoly may not be so comfortable in a year or two's time. Secondly, because as a result of these pressures, and the greater customer-awareness of business in general, Joe Q. Public is becoming used to a friendly and courteous voice on the other end of the telephone and to people who deal with him or her as a human being with choices to be respected. Even where they don't have any choice about whom to deal with, they are becoming more demanding of the basic courtesies.

I'd go so far as to assert that if you don't think of yourself as having customers, then in fact you don't know what your organization is supposed to be doing. You don't have that clear statement of organizational mission and values that is so important now. Take for example, the current interest in privatizing the prison service. The idea hasn't progressed very far outside the USA, but a number of countries are considering it. It's a useful example because a few years ago the prospect would have been unthinkable – a message to those who think of themselves in seemingly impregnable organizations. As soon as you think about privatizing prisons, you have to ask yourself: 'What are prisons for? Containment? Correction? Punishment? Whom do we answer to? What does a good prison look like, and a bad one? What should our standards of performance be?' If you don't have a body of customers in mind as the people you are answerable to, then the only performance criterion becomes conformity to the requirements of the system; and thus a symptom begat by bureaucracy comes to reinforce the bureaucracy itself. It's possible to think of quite a few organizations in this position – schools and educational institutions, many government departments, representative bodies, public utilities . . .

In darkest Yorkshire, between the two world wars, there lived a man who was paid ten shillings a week to polish the brass cannon by the village war memorial. After he had done this uncomplainingly for twenty years, he came home one day, flung his cap on the table, and said to his missus:

'That's it. Ah've chucked in t'job.'

'Eeh, I am vexed!' cried the missus. 'Why hast tha gone and done that, then?'

'Ah'm fed up being beholden to other people day in and day out. Ah've been saving up my sixpences, and Ah've bought mah own brass cannon, and Ah'm going into business for myself'.

One more point. If the organization resists the pressure towards customer orientation, then in the present worldwide political climate the chances are that the change will be enforced by legislation. Which means, almost inevitably, that it will be done insensitively; that more emphasis will be put on form than on function; that it will all happen in the dreadful glare of publicity; that opportunities for subtlety, and learning, are lost. I remember speaking at a large conference of National Health Service administrators, who were assembled to talk about customer care. I told the story of what we had done on the railway, and in the ensuing questions one woman began by saying that they were thinking of bringing in compulsory customer care training for all their staff, which would mean upwards of two hundred sessions, and did I think that the district manager should begin each course, as an earnest of their commitment to customer care? Instead of agreeing, for I could see that her face had fallen at the thought of asking for all that time from the district manager, I told the following story:

> When ScotRail started to concentrate on customer care, one of the first areas to be targeted was the telephone enquiry bureaux. To meet the required standards a large amount of investment in equipment and training was necessary. The first week that the Glasgow TEB met all its targets Chris Green, the general manager, appeared with a case of wine for the staff.
>
> Of course, the story lacks point unless you realize that previous general managers had appeared like the Fat Director in the *Thomas the Tank Engine* books, only showing up on official visits and going to look at the signal box and the train shed rather than the travel centre and the TEB.
>
> And the point was – still is – that for weeks afterwards that visit was the talk of the TEB; that the news spread around the rest of the railway like wildfire; and that if you want to put across a message to the organization, then hitting the gossip network is worth far more than appearing at a few conferences, or putting memos on the notice board.

Right. What can you do about it? What can you do to bring the organization back in touch with its customers? Like most of the actions in this book – like most strategies for organizational transformation – it's a *gestalt*, and happens best when there's a sustained attack on the bureaucracy, the introduction of enabling systems, and a generally coherent and planned approach. In particular, there are initiatives to be taken with customer contact staff, and supplementary initiatives with the back-of-house staff, and managers, who influence the quality of service the customer contact staff can give. Often you have to start with the customer contact staff, because that buys some credibility, but don't leave out the rest whatever you do.

Principles underlying a customer first initiative

Customers

- are best seen and heard rather than reduced to statistics
- are probably more on your side, and anxious to help, than you think
- can and should be consulted beforehand, rather than sold to or placated afterwards.

Customer contact staff

- didn't start life, or work, wanting to be rude/stand-offish/un-friendly to their fellow humans, and if they are it's probably our fault
- *may* need training in interactive skills, but almost certainly need training in how the organization works and how they relate to it
- are best fitted of anyone in the organization to represent the viewpoint of the customers within the organization, and are therefore also well equipped to produce product or service innovations if anybody thinks to ask them
- probably get more kicks than ha'pence, more blame than thanks.

Non-customer contact staff

- create the circumstances for the customer contact staff to manage, particularly those in pivotal jobs
- can be prone to interdepartmental fights, over-specialization, or other head office concerns which take their eye off the customers
- sometimes answer to other priorities than the customer contact staff.

Action on all three fronts together – customers, customer contact staff, and the rest of the organization – is more productive than doing it one step at a time, but one step at a time is how the measures have to be described.

Customers are best seen and heard rather than reduced to statistics. There is something compelling about the customer's actual voice: 'You ruined my reunion with my beloved' has more force than 'X per cent of customers' baggage is lost'. So, anything you can do to bring the voice and face of the customer in front of the organization is a Good Thing. The most amateurishly made customer video – talking heads, saying what they expect of you, what happens when it's wrong, how they feel when it goes well – carries much more impact than the most professionally collected statistics. Save the statistics for the marketing department; the staff in accounts and maintenance and service planning need to hear and see the authentic customers. Set up a few panels of customers; loosen them up with gin and peanuts; turn on the video camera and ask them to talk about what they expect, about good service and bad, about how you compare with the competition. Especially, persuade them to talk about what happens to the rest of their lives when your product or service works, or fails to work, as it should. 'This word-processor's not only speeding up my work, it's forcing me to be tidy' . . .. 'An hour's delay at one end of the journey means a four-hour gap at the other end' . . .. 'I don't have enough spare time to go running around every time my car breaks down'. Part of the process of becoming detached from the customers is that you come to see only that part of them that presents itself on your doorstep; they become a glutinous mass of bodies pushing through a checkout, a list of numbers in a phone book, the kidney in Bed Six. So anything you can do to illustrate the knock-on effect of a product failure for the rest of the customers' lives will add to the motivation to make things better next time.

Nonetheless, the customers are probably more on your side, and anxious to help, than you think. If you don't believe me, think what most people say about medical accidents: 'I don't want compensation so much as to make sure that it doesn't happen to other people'. Don't be backward about setting up a customer panel or two, or a users' group, or asking customers to come to conferences and be quizzed. The only caveat I'd offer is that it's best to invite a representative group rather than rely on the self-selected group that will emerge if you confine your invitations to your most frequent complainers, or to the existing statutory users' group if it exists in your organization. And if you do go out into the community and recruit a standing customer panel, for example, then in fairly short order you'll have gained a group of ambassadors for your organization, because you're hitting the local gossip network again.

If you have established a customer panel, or a users' group, then they can and should be consulted beforehand, rather than sold to or placated afterwards. Ask them for suggestions for product improvement. Consult them about proposed changes. Ask them how they'd go about selling the improved or existing products. The Mosaic Management Consulting Group in Bristol, with whom I work, do this as a matter of course, and it's nothing short of wonderful; the customer consultation meetings I've attended have saved us from putting out services under the wrong name; have produced good to brilliant improvements in the services themselves; and have always generated ideas for sales strategy and likely targets.

The most important thing to remember when planning customer contact initiatives with your customer contact staff is that they didn't start life, or work, wanting to be rude/stand-offish/unfriendly to their fellow men, and if they are it's probably your fault. A number of points to remember follow from this fundamental idea; for example, many of them feel offended if you offer a course in customer relations skills which implies that they are in some way deficient; they will certainly feel that way if you give the impression that all the organization's problems can be cured by half a day's training directed at themselves alone; that if the detachment from the customer has been endemic in the organization, many of them will have war stories to tell of times when the Old Spanish Customs in head office prevented them from giving what they believe to be good customer service; and in some organizations people may have drifted, or been redeployed, into customer contact positions, or have never been selected and trained for such positions in the first place.

Are you selecting, as customer contact staff (including those who will meet the customers mostly on the telephone or by letter) people who *like* people? Want to help? Have empathy? Technical ability is important, but it's not enough nowadays. I remember when I was in hospital there were two nurses who stood out as being at opposite ends of the spectrum. One was in the public hospital who, when I was too weak to walk, took me to the shower and massaged my back for me; the other was the sister in the private clinic who, when I was almost in tears after hours of intense pain, looked at my chart and said 'You've had the pain relief'. (By the way, there's nothing more frustrating than being an expert in sick organizations when you're lying impotent inside a sick organization.) I discussed the sister with her matron, who volunteered the information that the pressure on numerical performance standards was so great that the human qualities were left out of the equation; I went back to the public hospital and because Pippa wasn't there I described her to her colleagues: 'Slightly scatter-brained, probably forgets things, but full of love'. 'That's Pippa!' they said, and you could tell that they gladly put up with her slight scatter-brain and lack of method because of what she actually did for the patients, and for them. If they were all like Pippa, maybe the odd scalpel might be left inside a patient and sterner measures would have to be employed to ensure that they weren't; but the reality of most organizations is that we need to err in the opposite direction and make it OK for people's normal human warmth to emerge.

The best training for customer contact staff starts and finishes with the acknowledgement that we're all human beings; it may have a passage or two on interpersonal skills, but needs to be cast much broader. George Lafferty designs the best customer care training I know. He starts with a day of getting to know us and some of our foibles: games on perception and perceptual biases, the limits to information processing, and our tendency to stereotype. Then he moves on to communication: the skills of

communicating accurately, particularly when people don't understand, or are under stress, and the skills of communicating warmly
and with interest. Then he goes on to check product knowledge;
he finds that many customer contact staff are backward in coming
forward because they don't know their way around the organization's product range as well as they would like (not so bad if you're
selling commodities, but a real problem if the organization carries
a wide or constantly changing range of products). That takes him
naturally into teamwork, and there'll be some exercises to show
that we're all working for the same organization even if some
of us have different titles or locations; and because he tries to
work with a mix of functions in his groups, participants are able
to question the other functions and learn from them. There will
be a session on managing stress and conflict – most customer care
training ignores this – and sometimes one on people with special
needs. Then a senior manager will arrive to take questions, listen,
explain the background to things the group doesn't understand.
And, most important, the senior manager promises to come back
with responses to questions and suggestions within a short time.
His sessions are full of laughter. They don't seek to woo people
with fancy lighting and a chicken lunch; they're designed to make
a gentle and lasting impact, and they do. Years later, you'll hear
people talking about what they learned from George.

Where George scores, I think, is that he starts by treating his
trainees as Michelangelo treated his block of marble. He doesn't
see them as deficient people who can be cured by tacking on a
couple of techniques, but as people who get no kicks out of
sending away a dissatisfied customer, who want to emerge from
the marble block, and with the aid of a little enabling training
can be encouraged to do so. He doesn't insult them with the
implication that they've been deliberately doing less than their
best; instead, he lifts the veil on what a better place this would
be to work in if everyone were customer-oriented and then gives
them some highly professional help in overcoming the blocks to
becoming so. Part of what I admire in him is that he lives out the
values he espouses: his trainees are his customers, not his audience
nor his victims.

The customer contact staff are best fitted of anyone in the
organization to represent the viewpoint of the customers within
the organization, and are therefore also well equipped to produce

product or service innovations if anybody thinks to ask them. In fact, once you start any kind of customer care training you'll be deluged with such suggestions, and you'd better have a way of dealing with them. If the organization has really become detached from its customers, then the customer contact staff will have years of remembered pain to revisit: the times they had to turn away seven customers in a morning saying that 'we don't stock it because there's no demand for it', or picked up the phone to an irate customer who'd been passed from department to department before unloading his griefs onto them. There must be management commitment, at senior and local levels, before the customer care training goes ahead; local commitment so that you can get an answer on local problems, and senior commitment so that suggestions, complaints, innovations which need the release of resources or changes in policy can happen; and happen quickly. Without that commitment, the customer contact staff start to feel that they are being held responsible for all the organization's problems; whereas in fact once you start, you find that for every instance of a lack of skill causing a customer to be dissatisfied there are probably two or three based on lack of knowledge, or bad management decisions.

> A female flight attendant was being harassed by a drunken and lascivious male passenger. When she had finally made it clear that she was not going to retire to the back of the aircraft with him, nor give him her telephone number, he began to complain loudly.
> 'You're the most unhelpful, unfriendly, cold-hearted, stand-offish person I've ever met, and I shall report your attitude to your managing director.'
> 'And you, sir, are the most pleasant, helpful, and tolerant customer I've ever met. But perhaps we're both wrong'.

In most organizations the customer contact staff probably receive more kicks than ha'pence, more blame than thanks. We used to find on the railway, for example, that there would be four complaints for every commendation; more importantly, the complaints tended to be about the failure of the everyday service, whereas the commendations often came from people with special needs whom the staff had looked after particularly well. Not bad in itself, but what it led to was a feeling amongst the staff that customer care should be concentrated on people with special needs, when we wanted them to broaden their outlook to include every customer on every journey. Simply put, if the train was ten minutes late and there was no buffet, we'd be sure to hear about it, but if it was ten minutes early and the prawn sandwiches especially delicious there were no letters saying so. We addressed the problem in two ways: first, by instituting a system of service excellence awards (see p. 60). It's not only the principle of rewarding good service rather than punishing bad that's operating here, nor the principal of instant reward; it's also the meta-message that says 'When those Charlies from management are walking around the station, they're actually looking at us rather than sticking their noses in the air'. Albert Koopman sent 'Extra Mile' cheques with a little note showing Albert the Lion beating his chest with pride in his staff – it's the same principle. Instant, visible thanks; and the message to staff that management are interested, and the message to management that they'd better be interested. By the way, the bean counters go mad when you start this: they want to know what criteria you will use, and how you will account for every voucher, and what will happen if one manager has different standards from another. Tell them to go jump in a lake; you don't hand them out like confetti, and even if you did the total annual cost would probably be less than half that of a senior management inspection visit and a hundred times more useful.

The second action that helped the customer contact staff to receive praise for good work instead of kicks for bad work was the introduction of a proper performance review system. This is particularly important if you're the kind of organization where for reasons of shift-working or other causes people experience different supervisors during the course of the working month, and supervisors supervise shifting teams. Then nobody has the responsibility for giving constructive feedback to the staff; which means they don't receive it. ('Other causes' may include being the kind of organization that takes on part-time staff to cope with overload, or unsocial hours; such staff very rarely get any performance guidance and feedback, and yet by definition they're employed to be there at a time when the customer pressure is greatest. Crazy, isn't it?)

Turning now to the non-customer contact staff and management: those who create the circumstances for the customer contact staff to manage, particularly those in pivotal jobs. If I were putting together a bookbag for every aspiring manager's knapsack, it would include the classic *Up the Organisation*, by Robert Townsend; one of his gems is the admonition that everyone joining an organization should begin by serving customers, and should go back to this for a couple of weeks a year. This is the single best piece of advice in the business; everything else is remedial. The cost is as nothing compared with the unseen costs of employing large numbers of staff who have forgotten what a customer looks like, or needs. As Billy Connolly says, in quite a different context: 'Do these things!' Don't just stick them on the cookery book shelf and acknowledge their usefulness to some other organization – do it in yours.

However, what do you do with the non-customer contact staff already on board, the ones who rarely, if ever, come into contact with a real live customer? Several suggestions:

1 Show them the customer videos, which will have more impact on them than on anyone else in the organization.
2 Mix them in with the customer contact staff on every occasion you can, especially customer care training sessions.
3 Run as many team-building sessions as you can between the two types of job, concentrating on contacts between them on the lines of 'How can I, in my job, help you deliver a better quality of service to the customer?'
4 Encourage the 'everybody has customers' attitude, so that staff see their job as providing service to their internal clients rather than controlling them. This means more than memos and corporate videos; it means putting as much energy into internal customer care awareness-raising as you do into external customer care.
5 The managers of non-customer contact functions should be roped into as many customer contact activities as possible: serving on the shop floor, telephoning the customer who complains, going out with the customer questionnaires, interviewing for the customer video, setting up the customer panels. If they're scared, give them a bit of help; if they stay scared, give them a wee kick in the backside. Involve them in managing the feedback from customer care training sessions.
6 Lose no opportunity to write *customer awareness* into your organizational performance criteria. Make it every bit as important as the other criteria they have to answer to, so

that staff are encouraged to think: 'Yes, it is my job to monitor spending, keep the headcount manageable, decide where the new building should be, invest the company's money wisely – but always balancing those criteria against the criterion of customer awareness'. Try to avoid the situation where the person responsible for customer satisfaction has to fight it out with the person who holds onto the purse strings come what may; the fight, if fight there be, should happen in the mind of the person holding the purse strings. It goes into selection criteria; appraisal criteria; promotion criteria; failure in customer awareness is not seen as a tolerable fault. (One of our prize occurrences on the railway was a letter from a senior manager to a customer who had complained of the rudeness of a guard. The manager made the usual run of excuses and apologies, and then said 'We should add in his defence, though, that Mr Bloggs is a very good guard.)

I remember an assignment for a leading oil company. We'd made a study of the kinds of language and concepts middle managers used when describing effective performance in their organization. We interviewed two hundred, far more than strictly necessary, but there were political reasons. When we analysed the data, we sorted manually the cards on which the separate comments were written. Fully 30 per cent of the cards concerned correct relations with head office – knowing the systems and procedures, getting the paperwork right. Another 20 per cent had to do with enforcing the same performance from your own staff, and most of the remainder with highly cerebral analytical skills, and the skills of stress management.

Five cards out of the hundreds we collected, not 5 per cent just five, had anything to do with the customer.

Reviewing my own experience in customer first initiatives, I'm struck by two things. The first is that when I started to work in the area, I resolved to be a better customer myself; to smile more, engage eye-contact, praise for good service, say why I liked the product or service. Besides being generally good for my soul, I thought it would give me more legitimacy when I complained about poor service, or helped people give better customer service. What was amazing was the effect this resolution had on the average customer service person; there'd be a delighted smile and you could see that this one interaction had raised everybody's game. One conclusion to be drawn from this is the trite one that if everybody made a conscious effort to be 10 per cent nicer all the time, it would be a much better world, the second is simply how *easy* it is to get people customer-oriented.

My second insight is that putting the customers first can be as easy, or as difficult, as you choose to make it. It's a prime example of the David solution – customer awareness is not so much a skill in which people are naturally deficient as an attitude/skill which they have learned to suppress because the organization has hitherto not rewarded it. Chip away the blocks and accretions, and most of it's still there. After all, we're all customers. We know what we want from our own shops and suppliers, and customer care is simply a matter of doing unto others as we would wish others to do to us. Like all the issues involved in organization transformation, it's not one you cure by throwing money at, nor sending memos about; it has to be lived out, modelled, enabled. I don't have much time for the ra-ra approach to putting customers first. You know the sort of thing, packing two hundred folk at a time into a hall for a day's presentations; of course it produces a Hawthorne effect, but it doesn't tackle the roots of the problem – the isolation of customer contact staff, the organization systems that are not customer-oriented, the invisibility of the customers' presence when decisions are being made, and the career structures that make it possible for someone to work twenty years without ever meeting a customer.

I said earlier in this chapter that customer care initiatives are part of a *gestalt* – that it's a necessary but not sufficient condition for organizational transformation. This is true; but on the Enid Blyton principle of starting with the easiest knot, a customer first programme may be the easiest knot in the transformation process. It'll raise questions that demand answers; it'll often produce ideas for product and service improvements; it's visible, and like motherhood and apple pie it's difficult to object to. Just be sure, when you start, that your approach encompasses everyone in the organization; and be ready to roll with the rest of the transformation process when the success of the customer first programme makes people clamour for it.

8 The enabling organization

Doctors are fond of quoting that part of the Hippocratic Oath that begins: 'First, do no harm'. That's a good motto for the enabling organization. It doesn't get in people's way; it doesn't, consciously or unconsciously, convey the impression that if it's not in the rule book it can't be done.

One of the symptoms of a disabling organization is an over-reliance on form as opposed to function. I've lost count of the number of times I've been told of expensive consultancy exercises aimed at rewriting the organization chart – tales told by people who know full well that the reorganization didn't work, that it was a futile exercise in looking for the sixpence not in the dark where you dropped it, but under the lamppost because the light's better there (Stewart's Law of organization design: structural solutions to functional problems don't work). This chapter has a little bit (it's enough) to say about rewriting the organization chart; but mostly the job of building the enabling organization consists of working on the spirit rather than the letter. Working on the structure has to take place hand-in-hand with building the kinds of systems that will enable people to work within the new structure; with modelling by the transformational leaders, wherever they might be in the organization; and of course with the determined attempts to bust bureaucracy, regain touch with the customer, and work as if we were all in this together.

My favourite Garfield cartoon has several frames of our feline friend ravelling knitting wool, stropping his claws on the furniture, running up the curtains, playing with a mouse, and rolling on his back to have his tummy tickled. In the last frame he stalks off, tail in the air, saying over his shoulder: 'That should hold you cat freaks for a while'. Well, the next bit of the book should hold you structure freaks for a while.

Organization structure is important. And restructuring is sometimes a necessary, but never a sufficient, condition for organization transformation. To approach restructuring properly, it's useful to begin by considering the assumptions that were made in the days when Management by Objectives was all the rage. The assumption behind that system was that the chief executive was the person best fitted to plan, operate, and control the organization. In order to do this, he (and it usually was he, in those days) needed two things: access to all the information within the organization, and a compliant hierarchy of managers beneath him who would each take their share of the chief executive's tasks and implement them. The chief executive was the *fons et origo* of the organization; he had managers only because he couldn't do it all himself.

The enabling organization places the emphasis elsewhere: at the interface with the customers. They are the life-blood of the organization, and the staff who deliver the organization's products or services to the customer are identified as having their own unique responsibilities for the organization's survival. The role of senior managers in this organization is then best described by the single phrase: 'How can I help?'

How can I help you?

- by seeing that you're the right person for the job, and that you receive the training, coaching, feedback you need to do the job well
- by making sure that you know what's expected of you
- by ensuring you have the resources and information you need to deliver quality products or services to the customer
- by making sure that the boundaries between your job and your colleagues' are sensibly defined and don't become over-rigid
- by making sure that you're paid fairly for what you do
- by listening when you've got something to tell me, or to ask

and

- by handling the organization's resources so that it continues to prosper
- by planning and forecasting what sort of organization we need to be in the future, and what opportunities we should be taking up
- by shaping the organization, and setting the climate, so that everyone can give of their best and feel good about it
- by monitoring organizational performance so that action can be taken quickly if things start to go wrong.

This is the philosophy of the organization of the future. Some people have drawn it as an organization chart turned upside down, with the customer interface at the top, and the chief executive at the bottom. However you choose to draw it, say goodbye to the idea that some jobs are inferior to others; rather, they are different. When Cas Mason, my all-time favourite railway guard, gets onto a train full of stroppy tired commuters, or discontented football supporters, and charms them into having a good and peaceful journey, he's doing a job that his director couldn't do; and the perception of the customers is formed far more by what Cas does than by what the chief executive does. It's the job of the director to set the climate in which Cas can do his work properly; Cas knows that, and the last time I met him he couldn't stop talking about it. An enabling organization structure recognizes this relationship; simply put, it acknowledges that without the people at the customer interface there's no prosperity today, and without the people in the centre there's no prosperity tomorrow.

It follows that there are several principles underlying the design of the organization of the future. The first is that the organization is likely to be *flat*. If you read the lives of the great generals (or Norman Dixon's book *On the Psychology of Military Incompetence*, which is brilliant) you see that they often visited the troops on the front line. The bad ones, the ones who presided over senseless slaughter, stayed in their chateaux in the rear and ran the war from charts and dispatches. Part of the leader's job is to enable and inspire his or her people; it's more difficult to do this the more layers of hierarchy there are between the leader and the troops. How can the leader help if s/he is ignorant of the real conditions on the front line? Therefore, see how few layers in the hierarchy you can manage with. The maximum is five:

- customer interface staff at the bottom (or the top) of the hierarchy
- next, the staff responsible for their day-to-day co-ordination, feedback, information, coaching, resourcing, etc.

then at the top (or bottom):

- the chief executive
- the managers responsible to the chief executive for particular geographical or specialist areas

and, perhaps, in the middle:

- the managers in a large organization who liaise between top and bottom, translating strategy into tactics and inputting tactical information into strategic decisions.

with each given as much authority as possible to do the task in hand.

The second principle underlying the design of the transformed organization is that it is *fluid*. In other words, it is understood not to be set in stone; it may change. Equally important is the notion that changes are more likely to be evolutionary than revolutionary; in other words, you don't sit around in one organization chart for eighteen months and then all the boxes change and you conform to another shape for another couple of years. Of course, if the notion of evolutionary change is accepted, it follows that different parts of the same organization may have slightly different shapes on the organization chart. If the job's being done properly in all the different places, and there are no horrible inequities, it doesn't matter. Evolutionary change is, of course, much easier in the flatter organization, because people's vision isn't clouded by the complexity of the hierarchy; if relationships are simple, and levels are few, then any problems with those relationships are both more apparent and more easy to fix.

The third principle is that the organization design is *owned by the people who make up the organization*. You want a situation where people say: 'We understand how we are formed into an organization; we think it makes sense; we had an input into saying what shape it should take, and we know what to do – and that we're expected to do it – if for any reason the organization shape ceases to fit'.

This third principle is the most important of all. Some consultants will, I'm afraid, try to kid you into thinking that organization design is an arcane art, accessible to only a few, and extremely expensive. In fact, if you follow the principle that the best consultants are those working inside their organization, you can save yourself a pot of money and acquire a better organization design at the same time (by *better*, I mean one that looks good on paper and stands a good chance of working in operation).

How to tackle an organization redesign

1 Consult your heart to make sure that you're not relying on a redrawing of the boxes on the organization chart to do all your work for you. If you are, stop, and talk yourself into a change of heart.

2 Gather as much information as you can about the way the organization works now. Attitude surveys, climate surveys, customer responses, exit interviews if you've lost some top performers, or people who've gone elsewhere and had a more stunning career than they would have with you; case studies of notable failures and successes; studies of the style of your best leaders; organizational responses to change; blockages and innovations. Run this information through your brain and ask what it tells you. Talk it through, if necessary, with a disinterested outsider.

3 Organize some discussion groups. As many as you can. Ideally, the groups should contain a mix of functions and as much a mix of levels as you think will enable everyone to feel free to contribute. Agenda for the discussion group:

(*a*) a presentation on how organizations grow and change. (The model given in the Appendix is my favourite, because it makes heads nod in agreement and understanding faster than any other);

(*b*) a presentation on the key concepts arising from item 2 above;

(*c*) split the group into several smaller ones and work with them on envisioning the future of the organization. The 'draw a picture representing your ideal organization' exercise is very helpful here. Whatever catalyst you use, make sure that the discussion groups are physically active – lots of flip chart paper and magic markers – and that they begin by talking metaphor, values, visions. This is not the time to redraw the organization chart; it is the time to draw the future – as if it were a green field. When you've drawn the future, the organization chart will follow naturally, as form always does follow function in organisms which survive;

(*d*) ask the different groups to present to one another, and draw out the common themes;

(*e*) now let them work out the appropriate organization design to achieve their vision. If they object that they know nothing about organization design, point out that they actually know a lot because (i) they've worked in one, and (ii) they've probably grumbled about times when it was wrong. Tell them that the reason they think they can't do it is because it's a *simpler* task, not a more complicated one, than they think;

(*f*) take away the results, with a promise that you'll be back to them within *x* weeks. Compare them with those from all the other discussion groups. If you have severe dissent, call the dissenting groups (or their representatives, who will not necessarily be the most senior members) together to resolve the difficulties. Make sure, in the process of resolution, that you and they are not looking for a false symmetry or worrying too much about how to get there from here.

(*g*) think about how the organization will look two years hence once the redesign is in place. What sort of structures, systems, controls, will it require, and what sort of leadership and management? What do you have to do now to enable these things to happen? Start doing them;

(*h*) introduce the new design as a pilot, if you possibly can, in an area where you can be sure of intelligent support. Listen to the people who participated in the pilot. Send the results of your listening around the organization.

(*i*) go for it.

It's that simple. It's a process that respects the intelligence and the experience of the people who make up the organization; gives them a chance to dream informed dreams, and put those dreams into action. If you feel uncomfortable with the process, then I'm afraid you don't trust them enough. (Or they don't trust you, in which case go back to item 1 above and ask yourself what else you can do to make people feel that things really are going to be different around here.)

Message to personnel

That's almost all on organization restructuring, but may I have a word in the ear of any personnel specialists who might be reading this book? I find on my travels that many people nod sagely at the notion of the flatter, shallower organization; but then I start to talk about some of the implications that has for the role of the personnel function and it's obvious that not all these implications have been addressed. The three that bother me, because they do need action from the centre and they're not often getting it, are salary planning, career planning, and identifying management potential.

If you've been used to an organization where staff move gently up the hierarchy every two years or so until they find a nice comfortable niche which doesn't challenge their level of incompetence too much, then you probably have a book full of those nice ogival curves showing salaries levelling off after three or four years. Please re-write it; in the new organization staff may stay at the same level for much longer, and anyway you'll probably want to pay them on the basis of skills acquired and used rather than just for getting older, won't you?

As for career planning, the organization of the future has very little place for the old-style specialist, the one whose first loyalty was to his or her profession and guarded its boundaries with his or her life. But nobody joining you as an engineer is going to voluntarily relinquish a year or two's seniority and experience on the engineering ladder to go and work in the marketing department or on the sales floor. What are you doing about career planning to encourage more generalists, people who still have their specialist contribution to make, but also know their way around the other functions within the organization and have been trained to think across functional boundaries, not within them?

The final word to personnel specialists concerns the identifica tion of management potential, and I'll begin it with a true story in which only the names have been changed to protect the guilty:

> I was asked by a large organization to run a workshop for them on the latest techniques in management development, for their line personnel managers. We put together a programme that seemed right at the time, but when we actually ran it, the picture had changed; the stock market had (rightly, in my view) lost confidence in the organization, its shares were one-third the price they had been when the programme was commissioned, and we found ourselves running an ad hoc week working out strategies for how they could help the organization manage through the crisis.
>
> However, we still had some legacies of the old agenda left, and one of them was a visit from the firm's in-house expert on management assessment. It was, incidentally, probably the firm with the most assessment data on its managers in the whole of the United Kingdom, if not the statistics-speaking world. The expert described their pattern of management assessment: formal assessment programmes at at least three levels in the organization, psychological tests, a performance appraisal form that looked like something from a computer dating agency. When he'd finished, one of the personnel managers put up her hand.
>
> 'Let me clarify,' she said. 'You're saying that our managers get' and she enumerated all the different kinds of assessment 'and this has been going on for at least fifteen years?' The expert nodded.
>
> 'In that case,' she went on, 'why are we in the shit?'

I've worked in the area of identifying and developing management potential for more years than a woman should admit, and for all those years I've stressed the importance of getting the assessment criteria right: right not just for where you are now, but for where you want the organization to be in the future. It's no good getting together a wish-list of performance criteria, or picking them off a chart; even the usual forms of job analyses only serve to reproduce the performance of yesterday in the organization of tomorrow. The best way is to find out how people describe, in their own words, effective performance today. (There is a technology available – it's called Repertory Grid, fun to use, and a moderately accessible book on it to help.) Interrogate that description against an analysis of the demands of the future (very similar to the first few steps of the organization design process above, and you can combine the two). Then you know what kind of gap you have, and can guess at how difficult it's going to be to get there from here. It's a matter of saying, from the personnel department to the chief executive: 'None of your future business plans will fail, if we can help it, for lack of properly identified and trained managers ready to meet those new demands'.

Enough of the message to the personnel department. Back to the enabling organization as a whole, and to the second part of making it happen – designing and installing enabling systems.

If the organization's big enough to tire of its own bureaucracy, it's big enough to need systems and controls even after it's been transformed. Have a bonfire of controls by all means, but retain enough to keep the house together. But in the transformed organization the systems and controls are *enabling* not disabling. Definitions and examples follow.

Enabling systems defined

1   All systems enforce minimum performance standards. Controlling systems effectively place a ceiling above which people find it difficult to rise. Enabling systems have a different perspective: they set a floor below which nobody has an excuse for falling.
2   The systems are based on the assumption that people want to do a good job and are trustworthy.
3   The systems are expressed as far as possible in terms of principles people are to follow, not rules they have to obey.
4   The utility of the systems is judged according to how they help the organization deliver a better service to the customer.
5   The systems are minimalist, i.e. they control only those things they need to control and to a degree of control which is cost effective; they do not spend £1 checking whether sixpence has gone astray.
6   The minimalist structure overall is supported by checks which effectively take a micrometer slice through the organization to see whether there are any abuses or sub-critical problems. If found they are corrected speedily and visibly.
7   The systems place responsibility, authority, and information as close as possible to the people who need it in order to serve the customer.
8   The designers of the systems begin by considering how they should reflect and affect the aims of the organization. Only then do they go on to consider matters of form design, participation, etc.

9 The designers of the systems pilot them before introducing them throughout the organization, if this is at all possible.

10 The systems are designed to follow the natural rhythms and seasons of the business rather than to impose their own timing.

11 The systems are geared to respond quickly, or be bypassed, when there is urgent need.

12 The designers or owners of the systems have built in a procedure for monitoring how people react to them and whether they continue to meet the needs for which they were designed. A badly received system, or one that has become obsolete, is changed without fuss.

13 The system does not automatically stop people from taking risks or making experiments, and does not demand proof in advance that experiments will be successful.

14 A system that is primarily designed to promote dialogue between people should not be changed into one whose main purpose is to generate information for purposes of record-keeping and/or planning.

All systems enforce minimum performance standards: controlling systems effectively place a ceiling above which people find it difficult to rise, enabling systems set a floor below which nobody has an excuse for falling

In other words, do the rule-book and the procedure manual tell people exactly what to do (i.e. if it isn't in the rule-book the chances are they won't do it) or do they spell out the minimum they should do and encourage them to do more if they can? Are performance standards, objectives, job descriptions, and the like regarded as the limit on people's achievement, or the least that they and the organization have the right to expect of them?

The systems are based on the assumption that people want to do a good job and are trustworthy

Which most of them are capable of being. The chap in the accounts department, who has to have his work checked because the system says so, services his own car and trusts his kids to it; so does the woman who feeds her family by her own cooking. If people live long enough in an environment where their work has to be checked (or, worse still, where their decisions are frequently overturned by their boss) they stop giving their best, because somebody else will modify it anyway. Start trusting them, and see point 6 for more details.

The systems are expressed as far as possible in terms of principles people are to follow, not rules they have to obey

We dealt with this point in some detail earlier. Principles allow choice, discretion, room for maneouvre – all good things when you want to be able to deal with the unexpected. Only if you are certain that the demands of tomorrow will be the same as those of today can you rely on rules to carry you through, and in that case you don't need a person, just a computer.

The utility of the systems is judged according to how they help the organization deliver a better service to the customer

Customer first again. The best test is to imagine yourself having a discussion with a real live customer. Could you defend the system to the customer, explain how the system helps get a quality product or service delivered?

The systems are minimalist, i.e. they control only those things they need to control and to a degree of control which is cost effective; they do not spend £1 checking whether sixpence has gone astray

Sometimes, when I look at the mountains of data the average manager has to plough through, I'm reminded of Borges's story of the Universal Library. Borges, who wrote in a very spare style, takes you into a library which contains 26 letters, and nine digits plus zero, in every possible combination. Then he teasingly raises a few possibilities: that in here are all the proofs you would need of the existence of God, and their rebuttals; the most beautiful poem in the world, and the same poem with one word wrong; your own obituary . . . for me, Borges's story conjures up the description of the man who knew everything, but nothing else.
    Seriously, if you're drowning in too much data, something's

gone wrong. Either you're collecting too much, and a little judicious application of the 80/20 rule is needed – which is the 20 per cent of the data I need to tell me about 80 per cent of the problems? Or, the people who are sending you data need a little lesson in internal customer-orientation: would they please do a better job of filtering, or summarizing, or highlighting, or generally running it through their brains, before they send it on?

The minimalist structure overall is supported by checks which effectively take a micrometer slice through the organization to see whether there are any abuses or sub-critical problems. If these are found they are corrected speedily and visibly.

Sadly, not everybody can be trusted; and the 80/20 rule sometimes breaks down. With the time you save by not ploughing through furniture vans of data, and checking your subordinates' decisions, you run thorough checks throughout the system from time to time. If something's going wrong, put it right; if someone's breaking trust, get rid of them and make it known that's why you're doing it. Most important, do this quickly; this is what management by walking about is all about. This is a phrase which is much misunderstood: people take it to mean that managers should take a lot of exercise. In fact the emphasis should be on the word 'management': that by going around, doing the micrometer checks, the manager sees things that need putting right, and puts them right fast.

The systems place responsibility, authority, and information as close as possible to the people who need it in order to serve the customer

Because that's where they belong. The people who serve the customer, and their immediate managers (or sponsors, or co-ordinators, or whatever you want to call them) should ideally have enough responsibility, authority, and information to solve 80 per cent of the customer problems, and take advantage of 80 per cent of the customer opportunities, without having to ask permission. Misuses and mistakes will get picked up by the micrometer slice principle. If they can't respond to these demands, ask yourself if you've done all you can to train them, coach them, tell them what's expected of them, give them feedback . . . then if they still can't respond, tell them that you can't afford to carry passengers.

The designers of the systems begin by considering how they should reflect and affect the aims of the organization. Only then do they go on to consider matters of form design, participation, etc.

I wrote this part of the definition because I do a great deal of work in the area of performance appraisal and am so tired of finding systems that were designed by a committee getting together a pile of other organizations' appraisal forms and tacking a bit of this to a bit of that, adding a bit of the other, printing their version on different coloured paper, and launching it on an unsuspecting world. I'm afraid I have a nasty trick when it comes to talking about appraisal; I show people a 3×2 matrix in which the three rows are called 'control', 'maintenance', and 'development', and the two columns 'overt' and 'covert'. We have a discussion about which box we would like the system to be in; today, most people plump for maintenance with a bit of development. Right, I say, let's have a look at how your present system shapes up: the show-stopper is that you can say the system's about maintenance and development, but most appraisal training consists in coaching people how to have difficult interviews, and never includes anything about identifying and acting upon training needs, management potential, etc. The point I'm making is that so many systems, not only performance appraisal, are designed by starting with boxes on a piece of paper, or a draft form; and what I'm trying to do is encourage you to think of the system as a process first, and only then go on to think about the paperwork necessary to support it.

The designers of the systems pilot them before introducing them throughout the organization, if this is at all possible

I worked for a little while with a brilliant, if somewhat acerbic, man called David Brain; now sadly dead. David had designed a new system (I've forgotten for what) and was presenting the plans for implementation to his boss. The plans naturally included a pilot, but the boss wouldn't agree: 'You're paid to get it right first time,' he said.

David turned to the flip chart and drew a quick graph (see Figure 8.1).

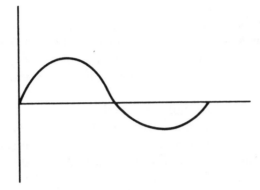

Figure 8.1   The best servo-mechanism

'That's a diagram of the performance of the best possible servo-mechanism,' he said. 'One error one way, one the other, and on line thereafter. Please don't expect a group of human beings to outperform the best servo.'

The systems are designed to follow the natural rhythms and seasons of the business rather than to impose their own timing

This is a simple cry of despair on behalf of all the organizations where work stops for a month because it's salary planning or performance review time, or because we have to spend to the hilt of this year's budget before we put in the next. There are occasions when everyone needs to be doing the same thing at the same time, but for every legitimate one there are ten imposed by someone in head office who can't breathe easily without having his or her next twelve months' work neatly laid out before them.

The systems are geared to respond quickly, or be bypassed, when there is urgent need

And the burden of proof, if someone wants to make a federal case of it, should be on the owner of the system and not on the person who bypassed it. There will always be unforeseen opportunities, or problems; if people have to ask for permission to act upon them, the moment may be gone.

The designers or owners of the systems have built in a procedure for monitoring how people react to them and whether they continue to meet the needs for which they were designed. A badly received system, or one that has become obsolete, is changed without fuss

This point arises naturally from the concept of customer-orientation, and of staff departments thinking of themselves as providing a service to their clients in the field. If the system does not help the line managers do their job better, change it. Don't punish them or cajole them into conformity; all that will happen is that duff data will be put into the system in order to keep head office quiet. Only in areas of financial probity or employee and public safety can you afford to be authoritarian about what sort of systems you use, and you wouldn't want anyone on the team who didn't accept these as important, would you?

The system does not automatically stop people from taking risks or making experiments, and does not demand proof in advance that experiments will be successful

It's the fleas and the tumbler again; spiced with the notion that most innovation comes unplanned, through serendipity (the art of profiting from happy accidents). People need to feel that if they spend a little of their time, and/or resources, pursuing ideas and innovations, they won't be called to account for mishandling company funds.

A system that is primarily designed to promote dialogue between people should not be changed into one whose main purpose is to generate information for purposes of record-keeping and/or planning

This point, like an earlier one, has its roots in my work with performance appraisal. How many times have you seen a system designed to encourage boss and subordinate to talk to each other become so penetrated by head office demands for information that the whole thing has become corrupted? (Test question: Which do you worry about more – appraisals that are done badly, or appraisals that are done late?) You can see the same factors at work in many other people-systems: briefing groups and attitude surveys can become similarly bent out of shape. Head office may eavesdrop, if the parties agree, but should not take over the chair.

Thus, the enabling organization. A frame, not a cage; looking to impose as little as possible; bound by shared principles and vision, enriched by constant dialogue; flexible; self-aware, and so in charge of its own evolution; committed to removing every internal obstacle to commanding its own future.

9 Teamwork for real

The scene is a river in the Lake District in the late afternoon. Three groups of managers are busy on their separate tasks. They're on a team-building course, and they're about to learn a lesson they'll never forget.

Here's how it came about. When they arrived at the training centre the day before, they split into small groups, with flip charts, and produced their own lists of the characteristics of a good team. You can guess the sorts of things they wrote: co-operation, mutual respect, clear objectives, shared resources, communication – the usual platitudes. They already work together – this group of twelve represented a cross-section, in function and job level, across one geographical area of its organization. So when they gave themselves marks out of ten on their own criteria, they rated themselves pretty highly. In fact, John Clarke, the area manager (a larger-than-life man whom I admire and respect dearly) gave me an earholing on the first night because he wasn't at all happy that his team should be thought to need a team-building course.

They've already worked their way through various outdoor tasks; today, after lunch, when they were all milling around in a cheerful group, we dropped into the melee three pieces of paper. One said: 'The task is to measure the depth of the river in nine places'. The second said: 'The task is to move a barrel from one side of the river to another, using the equipment provided, without the barrel getting wet'. And the third said: 'The task is

to construct a tower and a bosun's chair and transport the group
from one side of the river to the other'. Each task had the same
time limit: ninety minutes. After delivering the exercise briefs we
retired to one corner of the room.

With no prompting from us, they split into three groups of four.
Having kitted themselves out, the three groups walked down to
the river. The obvious place from which to measure the depth
of the water was by the bridge, so the first group stationed itself
there, where it found a good supply of essential and non-essential
equipment. A few yards up the bank was the barrel for the second
group, accompanied by some spars and lashings. A little further on
were the makings of a tower and bosun's chair, not over-resourced,
and one or two helpful diagrams. To Pete Bramwell and myself
(Pete's the best outdoor management instructor I know) it looked
as if we were watching three independent groups. From time to
time one group member would cast a glance at the others – a
glance that looked more like competitive checking of progress
than anything else. It's quite easy to measure the depth of a
river in nine places, so that group finished within about forty
minutes. They then strolled up the bank and watched the group
with the barrel. That's a task you can knock off in just over
the hour; so once that had been completed all eight of them
went to watch the group struggling to complete the tower and
bosun's chair. It wasn't particularly comfortable standing on the
bank – it was getting colder, and the midges were biting, and the
eight were quite pleased to leave the site after the allotted ninety
minutes were up. Amateurs can't build a tower and bosun's chair
in ninety minutes with the people and equipment we'd given them,
so the four people in that group were sad and disconsolate bears
when they made their way back to the centre.

Then we went into review. Each person was asked to come to
the flip chart and make three marks, one on each of the scales (see
Figure 9.1).

too little	**time**	too much
too little	**resources**	too much
too little	**people**	too much

Figure 9.1   Task review

And the penny dropped. It dropped first for Frank, who'd been part of the bosun's chair mob. Frank has a face like a wedding cake that's been left out in the rain, and every management quality except finesse, so I can't quote in full what he said but he turned to the depth-of-the-river group, and said:'You mean you were watching them before you came and watched us?' And then we started the real review, which finished at 0345 when the beer ran out. And what did we talk about?

> Who told you you had to be three separate groups, because you had three separate briefing papers?

> Didn't anybody spot the common denominator in all three tasks, namely getting across the river?

> Which tasks did you finish up doing three times between you, when you need only have done them once?

> Who said you couldn't share resources?

> Whence came the intergroup competitiveness which led to your not co-operating?

And most important of all:

> Here, you're all wearing the same clothes, sleeping in the same dormitories, and you said you'd left status and job titles behind. What happens, back at work, when one of you is an engineer and another is an accountant – some of you are managers and some operators – one of you is from head office and the rest are from the field? How powerful is that bureaucracy of the mind, much stronger than the organization's bureaucracy, that leads to the kind of thing we experienced this afternoon?

Unsurprisingly, they then uncovered all sorts of parallels between the afternoon's experience by the river and what went on at work. This particular group works for the railway: thus we saw the different engineering functions talking about how they could share possessions (this is when an engineer isolates part of the line in order to work on it) so that there might be one weekend's disruption instead of three; the engineers talking to the station managers about communicating more clearly, and earlier; and so on, late into the night. Between them, they now had plans which would save money; disrupt the customers less; incur less overtime; and probably reduce the collective ulcer quotient.

That particular exercise, and Pete's run it dozens of times, always produces the same results, no matter what kind of group is taking part. (Though we'll have to dream up something different now it's been published.) It illustrates one of the three key principles of true teamwork, which are:

- each **function or specialization** actively seeks opportunities to enable other functions or specializations to be more effective in the delivery of good customer service
- each **person** actively seeks to enable the other team members to work out their individual strengths, especially when the strengths are different
- in **order** to achieve a situation where alliances replace antagonism, disputes are settled by looking for the win/win solution, people make constructive use of differences, and thus the whole is greater than the sum of its parts.

In other words, teamwork involves different functions working together, and different people working together, so that each enhances the performance of the rest. It's the alternative to destructive empire building and internal competition between functions; on a person-to-person level it's the alternative to believing that those people who do not see things the same way as we do, or have a different scale of values or set of priorities, are automatically wrong and must be kicked and cozened into shape. *Our* shape.

For the rest of this chapter I want to suggest a few exercises which are good practical aids to team building. Most of them can be conducted by anyone with a modicum of skill and commitment; you don't need a degree in transpersonal psychology in order for them to work. What you do need is the necessary time and space; the team members present should cover a representative range of functions; and it's worth reviewing the advice in Chapter 4, p. 34, on analyses which lead to action. This will help you review and consolidate the lessons you hope people will learn. Obviously,

RED-BLUE EXERCISE

This is a game played in ten rounds. The **objective** of the game is for your team to **finish with a positive score**.

On each round you can either play **red** or **blue**. Points are then scored as follows:

If team A play	If team B play	Team A scores	Team b scores
RED	RED	+3	+3
RED	BLUE	−6	+6
BLUE	RED	+6	−6
BLUE	BLUE	−3	−3

You will not know what the other team has played on each round until you have made your choice, nor will they know what you have played. After both teams have made their choice on each round, the trainer will tell each group what has been played and what scores are.

There can be a conference after rounds **four** and **eight** if both teams wish.

Rounds nine and ten score double.

REMEMBER: THE OBJECTIVE IS FOR YOUR GROUP TO FINISH WITH A POSITIVE SCORE

it's a good idea to try them somewhere relatively risk free first. These exercises are all classroom-based. Then I'll describe one or two more of the outdoor ones which are particularly powerful but require more planning and specialist resources.

Exercise 1: Red-Blue (see opposite page)

This is an old chestnut of an exercise; it's been around for years, but it still produces results. Its objective is to prompt a discussion about the relative merits of co-operation and competition; how quickly a win/lose situation can deteriorate into a lose/lose; how easily people assume that they are in competition with one another. It's also about power, and about what happens if you don't communicate.

To play: **Divide the group** into two equal teams and give them the instructions (see Figure 9.2). Immediately, without answering questions, put the teams in their separate places, out of sight and earshot of each other.

Tell them that play will start in five minutes and in that time you will be available to answer questions.

Answer only questions about the rules of the game, not about tactics and strategy.

At the end of five minutes, show each team the prize which is available for their team if it meets its objective. **CARE: be sure not to say or imply the word WIN**. The best prize, unless you are working with a group of strict Baptists, is a bottle of wine or enough cash to stand a round of drinks. Don't do anything to imply that you have shown a similar prize to the other team.

Run the game, allowing two minutes (no more no less) between rounds. At the end of each round, after both teams have said what they will play, report the plays to both teams – in other words, in each round the teams make their choices without knowing what the other team has chosen. Do everything you can to appear as nothing more than an impartial record-keeper.

Reviewing

When you look at the scoring system it's obvious that each team can only be sure of reaching its objective if it helps the other team achieve theirs – in other words, by both playing red each time. The timing of the potential conferences is such that even if they find themselves in a win/lose or a lose/lose (i.e. by playing blue) they can recover, if they decide to confer. No two teams play the game in the same way: some will go red all the way, some will go competitive and then have a change of heart; some go competitive and stay that way, which almost inevitably means that you have to pour a bottle of good wine down the sink or set fire to some currency (it's important to do this, by the way – the loss may be small, but it has to be felt to be real); some break their word during the final two rounds. However it turns out, you won't be short of review material. Ten possible reviewing points out of literally hundreds:

1 What was all that about? – co-operation, trust, meeting your objective by helping the other team meet theirs.
2 Did they assume it was competitive? Why?
3 If some team members wanted to co-operate and some compete, how was that handled?
4 How was the decision to confer/not confer taken, and what effect did it have?
5 If one team wanted to confer and the other refused, what effect did that have?
6 If, towards the end, one group is positive and one negative, who has the most power? (The negative group can often have 'spoiling power' – we can't meet our objective but we can stop you meeting yours.)
7 If they agreed to trust one another, how easy was that to sustain?
8 Did they trust the administrator? Why/why not?
9 What would happen if they had to do the exercise all over again, right now?
10 Why do we so often assume that situations are competitive when we would achieve more by co-operation?

And, of course, go on to identify real situations at work which show a parallel.

Two administrative points: you may find that the teams take less than two minutes to make their decisions. Be sure to leave them the full two minutes though, because that's important time for talking strategy, or fantasizing about distrust. Also, you may find that some people have played the exercise before; unless they form a high proportion of the total, don't worry – it's another review point discussing how people who already have access to the winning solution manage to convey it to the rest. And you can always call the exercise Pink/Yellow.

Exercise 2: Card games

Whereas Red-Blue can be used to highlight personal and functional relationships, this one is primarily oriented towards functional relationships. It seems to work best with relatively junior managers or with managers who have close customer contact.

Give each person a small pile of cards. The instructions are: 'You may send one very specific message to each other person in this room, saying what s/he could do which would make your job of delivering good customer service easier'. A key ingredient is that the message must be specific – not the 'do your job properly all the time' kind of thing. Each person then collects the messages sent to them; if you maintain the silence long enough, someone will start to talk about his or her cards, and the work has started. This exercise is virtually self-running; your only job as a facilitator is to ensure that towards the end the participants begin to work out some job-related contracts on the basis of their discussions.

One administrative point: there are always one or two key functions who must be represented, because (*a*) they have a strong influence on everyone else's performance, and (*b*) because of this, if they're not there everyone will get into the blaming game.

Exercise 3: Case study development

This is based on the principle that often the best learning comes by teaching; it's also a good follow-on to the previous exercise, and together they can form a day that'll make a difference.

Very simply, you ask them to develop a case study, to be used by another group (use your imagination – it could be the next group, or an induction training group), in which a problem develops and each separate function adds something which makes the problem worse. Part of the macabre fun is that there is a strong element of real life in this: we've all been in situations where we've spent, say, six hours sitting on our ukeleles in a crowded airport lounge because the building maintenance manager forgot to tell the ramp controller, who didn't tell the customer services supervisor in time, and there's a consequent change of departure gate, and the crew rostering people don't do the necessary and nobody assigns extra staff to the check-in desks . . .

Again, this one more or less runs itself, and all you need to do is help ground the insights into work-related contracts.

Exercise 4: Rope square

A good one for stimulating discussion on the problems of communication within a team, especially when its members work in different locations or don't see one another very often. At least ten people are required for this one to work.

You need a long piece of rope (about 20 feet, enough to have the potential for a good tangle) and plenty of space. The rope should have its two ends tied firmly together and be coiled up.

Each member of the team is blindfolded. You then hand one team member the rope, and read out the instructions: 'The task is to form the rope into a square with all team members touching the rope'. The reviewing points are fairly obvious: how did they plan, how did they communicate, how did they ensure that everyone knew what s/he was supposed to be doing, etc. This exercise usually gives rise to a few good belly-laughs; like the time when, checking progress, the group contentedly heard five people claiming they were corners, and carried on regardless; or the time when one group member became so cheesed off with the process that he lay down on the ground as an act of withdrawal; forgetting that of course his message was completely invisible, and

ignorant of the fact that a sheep had misbehaved only recently on
his chosen resting place.

Exercise 5: Reef knot

This serves a similar purpose to the rope square, so choose one or
the other. Again a long piece of rope is required – not knotted this
time; and the more participants the better, because in this exercise
people often talk about too many cooks spoiling the broth.

Distribute the team members roughly evenly along the length
of the rope. They then grasp the rope with both hands. The
instructions: 'You are to consider yourselves glued to the rope
with super-glue; under no circumstances are you to let go. The
task is to tie the rope into a reef knot'.

A reef knot, by the way, is left over right and right over left, but
you don't tell them that unless it's crystal clear that nobody at all
knows this. It's amazing how many groups get themselves into a
glorious muddle before asking whether anyone knows what a reef
knot is.

Exercise 6: Chairs

Only for people prepared to risk their necks for high rewards.
Do-able with any mix of managers; the greatest returns come with
a senior management group containing a mix of levels.

You need a large room, empty apart from chairs, or cushions,
pushed towards the sides of the room at the beginning (and of
course the obligatory flip-chart for reviewing).

Tell the group that their task is to arrange the chairs/cushions,
and then sit on them, in such a way that the arrangement accurately
reflects their relationship in the organization.

That's all. And don't come running to me if your personal
accident insurance cover isn't high enough.

Exercise 7: Stabilizers and changers

The starting point for this exercise is a small, but reliable psychological instrument consisting of ten pairs of pictures (see pp. 114–15). The team members, working individually, are asked to decide which of each pair appeals to them more – working quickly, an instant decision is all that's wanted. Then they add up their totals of As and Bs, and chart the scores for each person.

The theory behind the instrument is that people who choose As tend to prefer stability, tradition, established ways of doing things, and people who choose Bs tend to prefer change, novelty, different approaches. In a large statistical sample you find a roughly 50/50 split between the two; the proportion in your team will depend on what kind of business you're in, people's occupations, etc. However, once you've identified the two types, and obviously discussed with the team to check that they feel OK with their own designations, there are various ways you can develop the theme.

Remember: the purpose is to illustrate that both preferences are valuable to a team or organization, and the ideal situation is one where As and Bs can contribute from their strengths.

One line of development involves putting As in one group and Bs in another, giving them the same tasks to do, and reviewing the relative success, and different approaches, of the two groups. In general, a B group will be more productive than an A group if given a classic open-ended brainstorming task; but an A group does better than a B group when given a task like constructing a lego-brick tower to a deadline. (The B group are often to be found arguing about which is the best of the many possible ways to go about the task long after the A group have sized it up and started.)

A further line of development, particularly fruitful after the team has experienced a practical demonstration of the different approaches of the two types, is to ask the two groups separately to reflect on *why* they chose the pictures they did – what sort of words, feelings, emotions, are aroused by the preferred and less preferred pairs. Then continue by discussing together how people with those preferences can make their best contribution to the team. The last time I did this with a group, they said things like:

What they liked about their own preferred pictures

A group	*B group*
Order	Pleasing randomness
Boundaries	Open-ended
Traditional	Unusual
Safe, secure	Risky
Symmetry	Unpredictability
Stillness	Movement
Realistic	Imaginative

What they disliked about the other pictures

Bs said of As	*As said of Bs*
Stodgy	Disorganized
Staid	Messy
Unexciting	Revelling in chaos
Formal	Unpredictable
Unimaginative	Unrealistic
Rule-bound	Playing around

It's not difficult to develop these themes in a way that makes it obvious that both change-oriented and stability-oriented people are necessary to the performance of a good team: those who innovate and those who see things through; the entrepreneurs and the good stewards of resources; those who remember the lessons of the past and those who look to the future; those who revel in a multiplicity of ideas and those who can filter out the unrealistic ones.

By the way, this is a reliable instrument for giving insight and promoting discussion, but don't use it for selection or assessment, please. And don't in your feedback, do anything to imply that one style is better than another – it's the mix, and being able to make use of the mix, that matters.

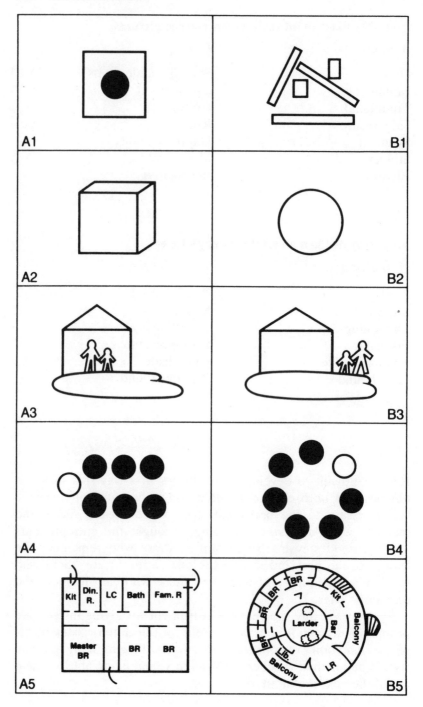

A1

B1

A2

B2

A3

B3

A4

B4

A5

B5

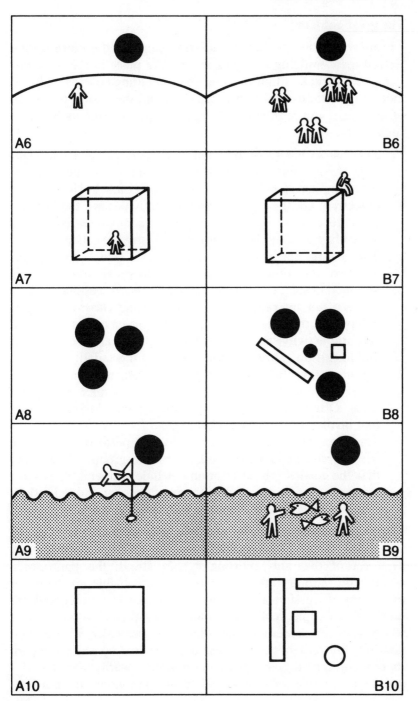

The great outdoors

I promised earlier (p.107) to describe some of the more sophisticated team-building activities which take place in the outdoors. Personally I reckon that outdoor team-building courses make far more impact than classroom-based ones, but there are a few words of warning if you're thinking of organizing or commissioning some such courses:

1   The course has to be planned to achieve particular learning objectives: what sort of issues do you want them to be reflecting on at different parts of the course? The learning objectives are the priority, and the activities are then chosen to achieve these objectives – not, as sometimes happens, a mixed bag of activities put together in any old order.
2   The reasons for using the outdoors as a vehicle for training are: first, the consequences of one's actions are more tangible and memorable; second, participants have to get involved, or be seen not to, rather than hiding behind classroom coping behaviour; third, it involves feelings and emotions as well as cerebral activity; and fourth, the memories are technicolour, and linger long after classroom learning has faded.
3   It follows therefore that outdoor management training should never be viewed as a test of courage, endurance or physical skills. Often the most striking lessons come during activities that involve little physical challenge.
4   The focus of reviews is not on physical performance but on the way the tasks were *managed* by the group. It's unlikely that the team's job descriptions include canoeing or making a rope square blindfold; but the management and team skills required have a lot in common with those at work.

Our river-crossing group, for example, also went abseiling, caving and hill-walking. The abseiling task was given to them merely as a set of diagrams showing a safe abseil; the appropriate equipment; and a time limit. It's an invaluable exercise for prompting discussion about how you persuade other people to take risks: people realize for themselves that if you're asking someone to do something that feels new and risky, it's no good pointing out to them that because they're wired up as per diagram there's nothing stopping them stepping backwards off the cliff – you have to work with their feelings and emotions. It's not soft, it's not optional, it's not pandering to weak morale – it's what you have to do if you want to get 'em over the brink.

Caving also brings out issues of handling morale and fear of the unknown; the need for contingency plans and communication; and leadership issues. I'll never forget the group who was instructed to do a cave survey, and planned on the assumption that it was about to enter an Ali Baba cavern; the expression on their faces when they saw that the entrance was a crack in the rock, best entered sideways, cannot be described easily. They hastily re-planned, and sent in an advance party of four thin people who said (on no evidence whatsoever) that they'd be back within about twenty minutes. The rest sat on the ground and pretended that their adrenalin levels were normal. Ninety minutes later the first of the advance party came out: pointing to three of the heavier folk, he said 'You, you, and you can't come in – you're too big.' They just about crucified him; twelve hours later they were still giving him ungentle feedback on the need to think about the mood of your recipient before delivering disturbing news. He was, by the way, far and away the most senior person in the group, but that didn't matter. And they all went in, and I counted them out and I counted them back.

The hill-walking task was productive, too. We split them into two teams and gave them separate briefings. The task was to work out a map reference and go to it, at which point they would find a clue to another map reference, and so on; the clues, put together, made a meaningful message. We also, without making a fuss about the reasons, equipped each team with radios. If you call the two teams A and B, then the distribution of the clues across the hillsides was:

A	B
B	A
A	B
B	A

AB

If the teams had thought about why we'd equipped them with radios for an afternoon stroll in the Lake District, they might have used them to communicate with each other. If they'd used them to communicate with each other, they'd have realized, because the form of the clues made it obvious, that they could each proceed in a straight line and collect each other's clues. They'd then have had a pleasant afternoon walk over spectacular autumn countryside, instead of a long slog and a final meeting which turned the air blue. All of which led to a review about communicating, co-operating . . ..

If you want to explore some of the issues of team-building in more depth, I can't recommend a better psychological instrument than the Myers-Briggs Type Indicator. This is a superb instrument which examines four fundamental dimensions underlying the way people make decisions: the first dimension identifies which is the person's preferred world – the external world of people and things, or the inner world of ideas. This dimension is called 'extraversion – introversion'; it is not exactly the same as sociability versus withdrawnness, because it refers to the *direction* and *focus* of attention rather than the noisiness with which that attention is expressed. The second dimension identifies the person's preferred mode of apprehending information: differentiating between those who prefer to use their five *senses*, and are therefore more reality- and fact-oriented, and those who prefer to use their *intuition* or sixth sense, and are therefore more oriented towards possibilities, novelty, complexity. The third dimension identifies the person's preferred way of making judgements: according to what is logical and analytically correct (*thinking-judgement*) or according to what fits the person's own individual value system (*feeling-judgement*). The final dimension identifies the person's preference for relating to the outside world in the mode of *perceptive* openness, or in the mode of coming to conclusions and *judgements*.

No preference is 'better' than any other; what's important is that people should feel confident with, and learn to use, their own preferences, and be able to choose situations in which those preferences can develop into skills; that they should also give other people the freedom to work out their own preferences. It is also a *developmental* instrument, in that it shows the way people grow and change as they mature and go through their life crises; and it is informed by a very clear set of values, one of which is that knowing your MBTI type does not put on you a ceiling above which you cannot rise, but a floor below which you have no excuse for falling – in other words, if according to the MBTI you come out as an ESTJ (an extraverted, sensing, thinking, judging type) then the least that you and the rest of the world can expect of you is that you behave like a good well-rounded ESTJ with confidence and trust in your preferred style; but you can 'play away from home', using other than your preferred style. Most of the other team-building instruments (and learning-style questionnaires and stress questionnaires) have their intellectual roots in the Myers-Briggs; however they always strike me as more like team photography than team development. Well worth having a look at.

To summarize. Team-building is about two complementary activities: getting individual people to work together better because they give one another permission to work out of their strengths and have learned to make constructive use of differences; and getting *functions* to work together better so that they have greater insight into one another's contribution and regard those contributions in a spirit of co-operation rather than competition.

Nonetheless, as I reach the end of this chapter and move to that on transformational leadership, I can't help thinking that the best example of team-building was when Christ washed the disciples' feet.

10 Transformational leadership

It can't have escaped anybody's attention that there's a new kind of leader about. Leaders who take their organizations, or their countries, into uncharted waters; who change what's done and the way it's done; who have an ability to reach out and touch people, inspire trust, try to make their part of the world a better place. They are clearly values-driven, and they're not satisfied unless they're making a difference.

It's no accident that we're seeing such leaders emerge now. The move towards the third stage of organizational growth (see the Appendix for a fuller discussion) brings with it a new emphasis on charismatic leadership, people and values. The reason is very simple; because in the latter part of the systems and controls stage of organizational growth the organization becomes low-risk, bureaucratic, procedure-bound, the move out of this stage into the stage of decentralization, de-bureaucratization, customer first, etc. – all the things I've been discussing in this book – requires that the leader encourage people to do things they're not used to i.e. to take risks. They have to abandon the safety of the rules and procedures and established ways of doing things, their notion of steady progression through the grades, the feeling of security in the arms of a stable organization, and instead do new things, relinquish some of their authority, abandon parts of the rule-book, come out of their offices and start walking the floor. And all this is uncomfortable, particularly for those who've had twenty years or so with the previous way of doing things. To persuade people to take the risks, to live with the inevitable discomfort of change, you can't hide behind the shaded windows of the company Jaguar, step into your private lift, and spend all day on the top floor shuffling papers; you have to be the kind of person people would die for, and that means personal contact, means a sense of charisma, means the ability to encourage, motivate, and – when necessary – command, on a grand scale. The new leaders have these abilities, thank Heaven; we need more of them.

The transformational leader:

1 Has a 'divine discontent' – things *must* change.
2 Hates waste and is always looking for opportunities to do things better.
3 Trusts his or her intuition.
4 Is excited by living with uncertainty.
5 Has a long-term vision.
6 Is hard-working and expects the same of others.
7 Is a clear, exciting, urgent communicator.
8 Isn't afraid to surround him or herself with able colleagues and subordinates.
9 Can use his or her status when necessary, but does not feel the need to pull rank.
10 Never stops learning.
11 Is clear about his or her values.
12 Is loved.

Has a 'divine discontent' – things must change

Most transformational leaders have reputations as a rebel, a difficult person to manage, a breaker of rules. Some have been fired for behaving that way. They can't help it – they're naturally change-oriented. The fact that something's been done the same way for years is, for them, a good reason for wanting to look for ways of doing it differently.

Hates waste and is always looking for opportunities to do things better

The classic definition of the entrepreneur, one who looks for ways of moving resources from areas of low productivity to areas of high productivity, fits the transformational leader. The difference between the transformational leader and the entrepreneur is that the latter usually concentrates on tangible resources, whereas the transformational leader focuses on people, and people in organizations; they want to move people's energy into areas of higher productivity. Whether by concentrating on people themselves, or on the organizational blockages that allow energy to be dissipated, they search constantly for ways of doing more, doing better.

Trusts his or her intuition

Intuition is the skill that allows us to apprehend information without relying on physical proof. Call it hunch or sixth sense if you like, but don't belittle it – intuition is a vital part of the transformational leader. The sense of when to ride the wave; the ability to run a quick force-field analysis in our minds and know where the pressure points are; the confidence to act on the sense that there is a logical pattern before us even if we can't now spell out every linkage; all these contribute to the transformational leader's ability to initiate action when everyone else is waiting to see how things will turn out.

Coupled with this well-developed intuition, by the way, usually goes a lack of interest in detail for its own sake. Intuitive people are usually so ready to move on to the next thing that they can forget to tie up the ends, or lose interest, which is one reason why it helps if they have a down-to-earth, stabilizing manager or two working close to them.

Is excited by living with uncertainty

What is unknown is also welcome. Wherever there is uncertainty, there is the opportunity to influence, change, make things happen.

The stable state is boring, past, done with, predictable; the transformational leader sees uncertainty as a golden opportunity for action.

Has a long-term vision

The transformational leader typically thinks a long way ahead, but not at the expense of making today better. Today is seen as the first step in many years of tomorrows. It's not uncommon to find them thinking way beyond the point where they themselves will have left the scene of the action. This is a Good Thing because the work of organizational transformation takes years; it usually takes three to six months before enough impact has been made for people to notice a serious and permanent difference; between two and five years to ensure that the vast majority of the organization is in tune with the new ways of doing things; even then the work is not finished, because bureaucracy has a way of creeping back. (As soon as there is a shortage of resources, for example, people tend to become low-risk and want to withdraw the authority they may have delegated away from the centre to the line.) In my view, there isn't yet a single organization in the world that can be sure that the transformation process has been completed. They may have crawled out of the water and on to the beach, but have yet to grow feathers and learn to fly.

Is hard-working and expects the same of others

They work themselves hard, and other people the same. They set themselves high standards, and demand the same of others. One of the characteristics I've observed in transformational leaders is their attitude to promises and commitments; they'd like you to say '*Yes*' to them, but if you really have to say '*No*' and have a good reason they'll understand; what they don't tolerate is the person who says '*Yes*' while hoping that the usual bureaucratic delays mean that they'll not be called upon to deliver.

Is a clear, exciting, urgent communicator

Dry, dull, and unforthcoming they're not. A transformational leader loses no opportunity of communicating the new way of doing things; face-to-face, on video, in writing. Face-to-face is where they do best: going out to talk to the troops, drinking hot soup with the night shift; making the time to make contact with as many people in the organization as they possibly can.

Isn't afraid to surround him or herself with able colleagues and subordinates

They want the best people working with them. They're not afraid to work with those who might outshine them in some respects. They recruit for strengths, forgiving weaknesses if necessary – it's easier to compensate for a weakness than add a strength that is not there. And in their dealings with colleagues and subordinates, they concentrate on successes, on opportunities, on things done well – though Heaven help you if you consistently let them down.

Can use his or her status when necessary, but does not feel the need to pull rank

I've described elsewhere in this book the leadership style I call the Mountbatten touch – the ability to relate to everyone, in a way that is unconscious of hierarchy, coupled with an ability to sport the medals and ribbons in order to encourage the troops by letting them know that they're fighting for someone who's earned their respect, or to gain respect when they represent their organization to the outside world. They have enough personal authority, enough authority based on knowledge and wisdom and vision and sense of accomplishment, not to rely on the authority of their position.

Never stops learning

They're often voracious readers. They have bounding curiosity about almost anything. They quiz people unmercifully, not as interrogation but because they need to know. They don't care who they learn from (and they know that the most useful lessons will often come from talking with the folk at the very bottom of the organizational hierarchy). They have the intellectual honesty to acknowledge their sources; they stamp quickly on any suggestion of the 'not invented here' syndrome.

Is clear about his or her values

Ask them why they're doing what they do, and they can tell you. And their answer is framed in terms of what they believe, what they value, what they feel impelled by. Somewhere in that value-system, you'll find a deep and abiding respect for other people, and a need to create a better world.

Is loved

Listen to their followers talking about a transformational leader, and you'll find respect and love not far from the surface. Love is a strong word – I could have written liked, or admired, or well-regarded, but I don't think they're a true representation of the way things are. They're too cerebral, for one thing; the transformational leader engages the emotions of the people who work with him or her. Spend some time with them and their colleagues, and the sense of affection and companionship comes through so strongly. I see it in their body language. They're open to hugs, and arms around the shoulder, and teasing, and laughter. Which leads to two quotations: first from Freud, who on his deathbed said that the only two things are love and work. Transformational leaders aren't afraid to mingle the two; it's part of how they are. And the second, from Lao Tse:

> The best rulers are those whose existence is merely known by the people.
> The next best are those who are loved and praised.
> The next are those who are feared;
> and the next are those who are despised.

> It is only when one does not have enough faith in others that others will have no faith in him;
> The great rulers value their words highly.
> They accomplish their task; they complete their work.
> Nevertheless, their people say that they simply follow Nature.

There are some truly appalling books on the market with titles like *Increase your Charisma Quotient*; I don't propose to spend the rest of this chapter emulating them. Instead, I'll assume that you, the reader of my slim volume, are a real or potential transformational leader yourself. If your first instinct is to shy away – 'No I can't, I don't have the clout, I've been kicked before' – please reconsider; I spend a good deal of my life being with ordinary people doing extraordinary things, and the world needs every transformational leader it can get.

So, I'll spend the rest of this chapter on a few meditations, musings, stories and anecdotes that might just help the transformational leader, whoever you are.

Go to the dispossessed for counsel

Often the best advice comes from people who have an interest but no personal stake in what you are doing. In most organizations such people can be found at the very bottom of the hierarchy – they see what's needed to give better service to the customers, they can still do an Emperor's New Clothes job on some of the sillier organization practices; they aren't afraid to speak up for fear of losing their pension. Interviews with young graduates, and exit interviews with staff you'd rather not lose, are one source of such information; but don't ignore the folk on the shopfloor.

Another group of dispossessed are the old; those about to retire, those who have retired. They often retain a loyalty to and interest in their old employer; they've seen changes come and go; they might have tales to tell of their own innovations that were sat on. They'll remember what it was like before the systems and controls bit hard. At the very least, they can put you in touch with some old values; at best, they'll be a real source of insight and wisdom.

> It's only partially relevant, but I can't resist telling the story of what happened when I did this with a group of old Great Western guards. One of them, Guard Salter, was asked to speak, through the video, to any new guard joining the railway. He began by speaking about the odd hours you'd work, and how you'd miss football with the lads, and Evensong, and Sunday Mass . . . and then his back straightened, and he said: 'But there's no other organization where you could be trusted to carry four hundred people through seven counties in a day, with nobody with a white coat and a stop-watch standing over you.
>
> 'And I'd also say,' he added, 'watch your language very carefully. One day, just after the war, I had a little girl lost on my train. I took her into the guard's van, and calmed her down, let her play with my gold watch, and then I wanted to know how to find her mother. Here I made my mistake. 'What's Mummy like?' I asked, and she said 'Guinness and Canadian soldiers'.

The third group of dispossessed are, of course, the customers. They can tell you a thing or two about the organization. Go on a Project Hear with the customers: not only the ones who complain, but the everyday ones. They know what it's like to do business with your organization.

The top-down strategy isn't always the best

The traditional style of passing a message from the top of the organization to the bottom is to start with the top talking to the next layer down, who then pass it to the next layer, and so on until it reaches the very outposts. Now we all know that this doesn't work very well with plain factual information. Most of us have played variants on the game in which the message 'Send reinforcements, we're going to advance' becomes 'Send three and fourpence, we're going to a dance'. When the message is not about facts, but of the new way of doing things round here, you can be pretty certain that it'll never filter down as fast as you want it, and in any case you don't only want the message to be heard, you want it to be acted upon.

A better strategy is shown in Figure 10.1

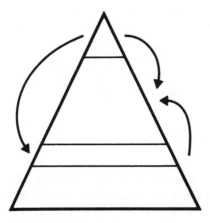

Figure 10.1   Pivotal jobs strategy

The diagram represents on the lefthand side the flow of energy from the leader and his or her team from the top of the organization down into the pivotal jobs: the junior managers and senior supervisors, the people from whom you receive the most impact on customer perception per square foot of person employed. Even a transformational leader has limited energy, and the organization has limited resources. Focus that energy on the pivotal jobs, particularly those low down the organization, and you achieve two things. First, a chance of influencing the young people, those who have not yet been frozen by the bureaucracy, the people who still have years and energy to give to the organization. Second, you then produce the pressure shown on the righthand side: pressure from above and below on the corporate concrete, on the custodians of the word '*No*' in head office. It's like military strategy. You secure your beach-head (a committed group of staff working around you) and then you proceed to secure your lines of supply. I promise you, this recipe works a great deal faster, and produces better results, than the top-down strategy.

But it has a price, one that the true transformational leader won't be afraid to pay. The price is that the leader, and the top team, have to be in direct contact with those in the pivotal jobs. In practical terms, you may want to run a series of discussion groups, or envisioning groups, or training sessions, with them. In those sessions they'll pick up the message that you want them to start doing things differently. You don't want them leaving you with the thought that 'It's all right for you, you're your own boss, but I've got to go back to work for She Who Must Be Obeyed in Woop-Woop'. You need them to know that you'll be passing through Woop-Woop fairly frequently, and that you'll be having a word with them, and if there are battles they really can't fight then you'll have a few words in the ear of said She.

Training

'We don't spend enough money on training' is one of those cries uttered all over the English-speaking world; everywhere I go I'm presented with the report of some august body comparing the amount my host country spends on training with that spent in Germany, or Japan, or Korea, or whoever the nearest threat is. It also seems to be one of those problems that most people are content to live with most of the time. The trouble is, of course, that you can rarely prove that the organization's going bust for lack of good training. The symptoms show, but hindsight rarely points to the cause.

Train and train and train – particularly if you're the kind of organization that hitherto has judged itself on other than business criteria – a hospital, a government department, a local or national monopoly supplier. When we looked at the kind of training for managers on the railway, we found that it was all about running railways, and nothing about running a business. It's the same in hospitals, telephone companies, airlines, water boards . . . once we offered training in how to run a business, the performance picked up almost immediately.

This book contains several suggestions for ways of envisioning the future and comparing it with what we have now. Any of them will generate training needs. Bully a training organization into giving you exactly what you need, tailored to your own requirements and explicitly linked to the organization transformation. The pivotal job layer, in particular, will respond to an intensive training effort – not necessarily at first, but once you have a critical mass of people who expect 10 per cent more from one another you'll be well on target.

Hearts and minds are important

I can't make this point too strongly. You don't transform an organization by sending memos and corporate videos telling people that things will have to be different; you do it by being alongside them, working with their fears, giving them a hug when they get it right, forgiving the occasional mistake, sharing their journey. You do it by helping them talk about visions and values, rather than policies and procedures. It isn't always easy:

> I was working in a big government department that had recently absorbed a smaller one. The two departments had very different values and were composed of very different people. I had given my chat to the senior officials of the larger department, about organizational transformation; heads nodded in agreement when I talked about the importance of hearts and minds.
>
> Then one of them related what had happened to him the previous week, when he'd been to the wake that the smaller department was

having. They'd cracked a few tubes, and weren't backwards in coming forwards when they had a chance to tell him what they thought of him. He was obviously badly shaken and sore, and felt personally hurt and insulted.

'Sorry,' I said, 'but that's what I meant when I talked about hearts and minds. You didn't have much business being there in the first place, but as you did turn up, then you should have been prepared to take the heat of how they felt. Most of the time, working with hearts and minds doesn't hurt, quite the opposite, but from time to time you have to confront the fact that people are angry with you and you'd better let them express it.'

Modelling

Live out the values you espouse. If you're asking others to take risks, be seen to take bigger ones yourself. If you're asking others to work harder than they've done in their lives, work alongside them (and then take them and their families away for the weekend). If you're asking others to let go authority, don't go checking up on every decision they make. Give your decisions quickly – don't use your power to keep people hanging about.

Viv Read told me of the time she joined the Hunter Valley Water Board as a personnel manager. On her desk was a very thick file relating to two engineers whose jobs brought them into constant contact with the public; they wanted permission to wear a somewhat smarter uniform as befitted their position in public view. The file had been going backwards and forwards within the department for eighteen months.

Viv is known for expressing herself strongly, and she did so on this occasion, writing words to the effect that if nobody could tell her within twenty-four hours what cataclysmic effects would result from her agreeing to this proposal she would give it the OK. This she then did.

The following morning, she found a trolley and a half of similar files waiting outside her office. 'Now there's someone around who's prepared to take a decision, we thought we'd strike while the iron was hot,' said her staff when she asked where they came from.

The message the transformational leader conveys is not 'Do as I say', but 'Do as I do'. It should be possible to reconstruct the whole philosophy of transformation by observing the leader in action.

The Old Testament could be thought of as a procedure manual: here are the rules to follow. (The good news is I've got them down to ten;

the bad news is, adultery's still in.) The New Testament is different: here is the person who is to be the model.

Which is the more inspiring, and stays longest in people's hearts?

What to do when people break trust

Which some of them will do. Once you start thinking about floors rather than ceilings and frames rather than cages; once you indicate that you prefer principles to rules; once you delegate authority – someone, somewhere, will look to see what they can get away with. This is one of the uglier reasons why you need to back up the enabling systems with a series of micrometer-slice checks and quick remedial action.

If it happens, your first thought should be for all the others in the organization. Put yourself in their shoes. Think how they must be feeling. They'll be expecting you to come in with the big stick, take back some of their freedom, start looking for scapegoats. Those who reacted responsibly and well to the trust you put in them will be thinking that now the party's over and they go back to being pen-pushers. Use this time, right now, to help them realize that you don't intend to let one failure spoil a record of successes. If you play it right, you can come out of this with a strengthened team, and an organization which understands that trust-busters don't get a second chance around here. And you can look to them for support during the inevitable unpleasant interviews with your boss, or the media.

I remember one transformational leader who had to cope with a particularly unpleasant breach of trust. I saw him a few hours after the news had broken, and he looked as if he'd had a heart attack. I put the episode under the bell-jar of memory, knowing that the present pain wouldn't stop his concentration on building an organization in which the vast majority of people felt enabled to give their best because they were trusted to do a good job. What I hadn't allowed for was the next stage of the process, when he had to go into a meeting with a group of people way below him in the organization and half his age. Somehow, they had heard about it; and when I saw them with him, I was reminded of nothing more than a school of dolphins clustering around a sick schoolmate; gently but firmly they bore him up, caring for him, not overwhelming him but with exquisite tact and lack of patronizing they restored his energy and faith.

This story illustrates for me the importance of the effect the leader has on his or her subordinates. There's an episode towards the end of *The Cruel Sea* where Lockhart looks after his captain after the captain's been on a well-deserved appointment with oblivion; Lockhart undresses the man he's served under for the length of the war, tucks him up for the night, all the while talking to him and finishing by telling Ericson he loves him. Captain opens one eye: 'I heard that'. Lockhart: 'That's all right, sir, I meant it'.

Trust doesn't come quickly. You can't undo the effects of years of sour industrial relations or connived-at skiving, of the disempowering effect of not being able to take significant decisions, with a few weeks or even months of acting out the trust. The cock is always ready to crow three times. All I can say is that it's worth the effort; you can't do without it; and if you have dark moments, then some of the people you've released will be there to give support. And the true transformational leader, lacking in status-consciousness, unafraid of his or her colleagues, able to learn from even the blackest bits, will accept that support gladly for the sake of the future remaining to the rest of the team.

Another story from the Maori

The pressure towards biculturalism in New Zealand is strong and becoming stronger; many organizations are trying to make it work. However, one of the most frequently voiced objections is that the Maori people take ages to make decisions; they have to convene on the marae, and hold a *hui* – a long, formalized discussion in which everyone may have his (and sometimes her) say and the aim is consensus no matter how long it takes.

I felt able to raise this with my friend Waereti. 'What do you do when you have to make a decision in a hurry – a war, an accident, some other form of crisis?' What she said set me rocking on my heels. 'From time to time we all spend a night together on the marae in total silence. When you have spent the night in silence with other people, using all your other senses for perception and communication, you know what you can ask of them. You know the front and the back and the sides and the roof of their strength, and your collective strength. And, of course, you do all this under the eyes of your ancestors, and in guardianship of your own future, and that of your children'.

I'd been expecting her to tell me about a particular flag they ran up, or a new way for the chairman to open the meeting. I felt very, very small.

It probably wouldn't be appropriate to mimic this directly in a Western organization, though I'd take a small bet that the results would be surprising once people recovered from their initial self-consciousness. But the spirit of her story has something to say to the transformed organization. If work becomes fun again, which is one of the goals, then the line between work (awful) and home/family/relaxation (enjoyable) ought to become blurred. People who work together can also relax together; people who have noisy rumbustious meetings can also go to a concert together; people who meet during a business lunch might also meet for Sunday afternoon tea and a game with the kids. Above all, and this is the spirit of what Waereti had to say, people can learn to meet one another as people, rather than as inhabitants of confining boxes on the organization chart.

Short quotes to stick on the wall and read when the going gets tough

Or quote to other people when it gets tough for them:

The only thing we have to fear is fear itself.
(Franklin Roosevelt)

Courage is grace under pressure.
(Ernest Hemingway)

No more good must be attempted than the people can bear.
(Thomas Jefferson)

Having precise ideas often leads to a man doing nothing.
(Paul Valéry)

Form is a diagram of forces.
(D'Arcy Wentworth Thompson)

We haven't got the money, so we've got to think.
(Lord Rutherford)

Living movements do not come out of committees.
(John Henry Newman)

A committee is a cul-de-sac down which ideas are lured and then
quietly strangled.
(Sir Barnett Cocks)

Don't bite my finger – look where it's pointing.
(Warren S. McCulloch)

That which is not good for the beehive cannot be good for the bees.
(Marcus Aurelius Antoninus)

All composite things decay. Strive diligently.
(The Buddha)

11 Values and principles

Five years ago you wouldn't have found this item on the organizational agenda. True, there were a few organizations who sported the Seven Corporate Beliefs, or Nine Company Superstitions, on plaques on the wall by the potted plant; but in most cases they influenced people's behaviour only at the margin, giving a slight feeling of virtue comparable with cleaning your teeth at night as well as in the morning. At the time I knew only one organization which made a sincere attempt to live out its espoused values day to day (and even there the values didn't penetrate completely); I had tremendous respect for the effort it took for people to run a big company without, say, telling the littlest white lie in negotiations, or being able to strike a special overtime rate when the equipment broke down while they were completing a special order.

Things have changed; things have polarized. We have Gordon Gecko being cheered for his 'Greed is good' speech in the movie *Wall Street*; on the other hand we have all the initiatives with names like 'People first, customer first, quality first'. Look what's happening to corporate advertising: it used to concentrate on matters of size and clout; now it's moving to express values of service, excellence, quality – with some Japanese companies even making a point of their good industrial relations.

You can't transform an organization without asking the question: 'What sort of organization do we want to be?' and that raises

135

the issue of values. You can't ask people to start behaving in a new way without, at some point, having a conversation which appeals to their ideals; you can't prove in advance that every step on the transformation journey is charted and guaranteed successful, so you have to appeal to their spirit rather than their sense of security. (Anyway, we all know from bitter experience that 'The motivation is that you can keep your job' doesn't work most of the time.)

So, what to do about values? The transformational leader needs a clear sense of his or her own values, and loses no opportunity to communicate them through action. But I'd advise against writing them down and posting them on the notice board; from the rest of the troops you're likely to get a mild expression of interest – 'Oh, is that what we value today then?' as they pass on the way to the canteen. I saw a good example of this when working with a railway overseas. The chief executive had drawn up a values statement which said that the organization put its customers first, tried to run itself on good business lines, and was committed to continuing service improvement over the whole of its terrain. This was proudly presented to me as evidence of the organization's progress. When we did a thorough survey of the criteria people actually used in evaluating their colleagues' and their own effectiveness, however, the values were rather different: being technically competent, looking busy when the boss was around, achieving seniority, and voting for the right political party (or having the right religion, which amounted to pretty much the same thing. Planned service improvements had a remarkable correlation with local voting patterns, as did the newspapers in which artisans' jobs were advertised). The values had been imposed rather than derived, and those managers who had seen the document regarded it as of little importance.

Better to engage the whole organization, or as much of it as you can, in a values clarification exercise. I've already suggested some; I like the process of drawing a picture of the organization as you would like it to be. I've seen other consultants introduce into a values workshop a session where people have to say what animal the organization reminds them of, and why. Or model it with clay, or make a collage . . . anything to get out of analysis and into the realm of emotions and impressions.

But it's not enough to clarify the values; you have to put them

into action. You have to ensure the kind of climate where anybody
– *anybody* – can call a halt because what's happening contravenes
the company values. Where the newest recruit to the production
line can make a fuss when s/he sees an example of poor quality;
where salespeople are told not to make false promises; where there
are no back-handers, and people automatically return expensive
Christmas gifts; where nobody even dreams of using insider
information, and efforts to prop up the share price during a
takeover battle are unthinkable.

Consider the following case study:

> In South Africa there's a building society called The Perm. Afrikaner-
> run, it's one of the biggest, and something of an institution. Some time
> ago, the top management held a conference on creative contributions
> to the inevitable political transitions in that troubled country. Nobody
> wanted bloody revolution and a descent into years of trauma. One way
> of avoiding this, they thought, was to encourage amongst the black
> population the creation of a classic middle class, i.e. a substantial
> group of people who were prepared to invest in their future through
> education, saving, house purchase etc.
>
> They could help, they decided, by setting up offices in the townships
> and offering free banking. Mr and Mrs Nkosi could deposit ten rand
> on Monday and take out eight on Friday, and it would cost them
> nothing.
>
> The effect this had was nothing short of phenomenal. In a township
> riot, you'll usually find a few people standing guard over the Perm
> office, which is not to be touched. Their advertising slogan 'You are
> the Perm' is one of those rare advertisements which states a truth
> rather than an aspiration.
>
> But: the Perm is in competition with other building societies, who
> have not followed its lead. As a consequence, its costs are higher.
> The stock market, which does not place a value on far-sighted
> philanthropy, took a dim view of the reduced profits.
>
> Early in 1988 there was a debate about whether to introduce a 50
> cent transaction charge. What would you do?

Here's a few examples of values statements from organizations in
the transformation process. Read them, and if any appeal think
how your organization could put them into practice. Think about
the video test: 'What could we capture on video to demonstrate
this particular organizational value in action?' I don't promise that
it will be easy, but it must be done.

Some organization values to think about . . .

People matter

                        We don't criticize the competition

                                                Equal opportunities

                        Quality comes first

Everybody carries boxes

                        Honesty in all
                        our dealings

                                                Security of employment

                   Being a good citizen
                   in our local/national community

Encouraging innovation

                        Involving people in
                        decisions affecting their lives

                                                Customers come first

                   Recognition of good work

Concern for the environment

How will you ensure that every function in the organization reflects those values? That in every situation, especially the toughest, people will stick to their values? That occasions when people have respected the values will be noised abroad with praise, and occasions when they are contravened will be seen as occasions for mourning? That every plan, and every proposal, will be tested against whether it is informed by the values? What are you going to do to make sure that the values are lived out in a competitive bidding situation? A tough union negotiation? Redundancy? A takeover battle? An all-round budget cut? A claim by people damaged, or offended, by your product? When you know your competitors have a better product for a particular customer's needs? When a stroppy shop steward threatens a strike just before an important delivery date?

I've seen some lovely examples of values being lived out. The Rural Bank in New Zealand was given about nine months to find itself a buyer; Vance Hainsworth, the personnel director, put together a plan to ensure that as far as he could help it, nobody would be made redundant after the sale for lack of proper training. Hours after the train crash at Clapham Junction in 1988 British Rail announced that they admitted full liability and would bend over backwards to help families affected (and how good it was to see the recognition that action received in the popular press: John Biggs, the claims manager, does an unpleasant job in a way that models values in action); a senior manager and a junior operator from Argyle Diamond Mines in Australia sharing a platform to talk about how that company lived out its pioneering approach to industrial relations, the manager working the slide-show for the operator, both of them delightfully unaware of the impression their obvious commitment made on the audience. (It contrasted sadly with the presentation from an American union leader, and led my Danish neighbour to whisper, in a delightfully up-and-down voice: 'I am reinforced in my belief that I only need to visit the States every ten years; I am missing nothing by not going more often'.)

So far, I've written about values as if they were all nice ones. They're not. It's obviously possible to run an organization on some really nasty values, and every time there's a stock market crash or a City scandal some more come to the surface. One large UK company spends half a day, as part of its management training, telling new managers why it's company policy to pay its suppliers between six and eighteen months after the bills have come in.

Yuppie triumphalism; we're big enough to push the little guys around; the principle of deniability; damaging internal conflicts fomented by top management under the guide of creative tension – all these and more are values that you can see lived out, with more or less explicit acknowledgement, every day. It would be good to be able to say that their days are numbered. All you can say with certainty is that the energy they have to put into reinforcing those values saps the strength of the organization; this contrasts with the energy that is released within an organization informed by transformational values. The guy in the white hat may win in the last reel after all, because he's not having to look over his shoulder quite so often for fear of betrayal.

Maybe I can finish by sharing some of my own values and beliefs; after all, this has been a very personal book, based on my own belief that the old-style rule-bound bureaucratic organization has had its day, and that those of us who care had better start building different ones.

I believe that ordinary people can do extraordinary things. One of my sharpest learning experiences ever was listening to Mary Ross describe her efforts to develop an intelligence test that would more accurately reflect the abilities of those people whose intelligence is expressed through action rather than analysis: the school children who don't respond well to being told to sit in a corner and read a book; the kids who need to be involved, who don't know what they're thinking until they've heard themselves say it; who don't easily fall in love with the pursuit of abstruse knowledge for its own sake but need to have a purpose in mind first. Mary had run a group of Glasgow housewives through the Myers-Briggs Type Indicator, and given them feedback. Most of them fell into the bottom lefthand corner of the chart, which Myers-Briggs aficionados will recognize as the extraverted sensing types – in other words, oriented towards action rather than analysis. During that feedback session, some of the women pointed to the top righthand corner – the introverted intuitives, the ones who are most at home with analysis and symbolic processing and all the things the classic intelligence test esteems. 'You mean they're the clever ones?' they asked. And Mary, impassioned, crying out: 'No. They're the academic ones. You're clever too – you're the ones who have to bring up four kids on what you get from the DHSS, who have to get the shopping home somehow with a push-chair and a toddler when the lifts have broken down, who have to manage when your man's out of work and goes on the drink to forget . . .' Mary's cry opened my eyes to the achievements of people whose giftedness lies in a different sphere from my own. And I find that the more I look, the more I have learned, and the more I regret that right from the first days in school the abilities of these people – and they amount to a good 35 per cent of the population – have been regarded as second class.

I veer between deep despair and extraordinary faith when I look at the struggle between good and evil that goes on in the world. There's the nagging little devil who, even as I wrote about the possible triumph of the man in the white hat, whispers Gresham's Law: 'Bad money drives out good'; and asks me to apply that to the discussion of corporate values; who points out the apparently self-sustaining obstacles to change in aspects of our political or social systems; the stock markets which need feeding with good annual reports, so that people concentrate on the figures rather than the quality; the electoral terms which mean that it's difficult to challenge the established way of doing things in bursts of longer than eighteen months to three years, and place the real power in the hands of civil servants; the disgusting electoral system that places the leadership of what we used to call the free world in the hands of the person who can pay for the most aggressive sound bites. Surely I can't be the only person who, on going into a dealing room, wonders whose foot on what shovel is represented by the green figures which apparently spell doom or triumph? and what would happen to the whole *kartenhuiskerfuffle* if a mouse farted near a terminal in Reykjavik and thereby inserted duff data into the system?

The faith comes back, and sustains, when I look at what people *do* manage to accomplish. At the great examples of organization transformation that we *can* see around us; the people who lead them, and the response they receive from the rest of the troops. At the leaders who emerge from time to time and change the way the world thinks, from Geldof to Gorbachev. It comes from the ordinary folk in organizations going through the transition process, and their naive delight in what's happening to them. When the going gets really tough, I recall to mind a night spent with a group of the lads from Network SouthEast, talking and laughing about what was happening, celebrating one another, hugging – the sense that one was part of a process that was unstoppable. It comes, too, from seeing in action overseas a value rarely openly espoused in the old world – the love of country and the sense that everyone can make a contribution.

In March 1987 I taught a short course on organizational development at the University of Cape Town, as part of their MBA programme. The students were in their mid-twenties; a mixed bunch (yes, black and white), all in full-time employment. They had to do a project back home as part of their qualifying process. So, on the last day, we had a session to decide what projects they would choose. To start with, like students everywhere, they decided to do their normal jobs but write about it. I encouraged discontent with this approach, as insufficiently challenging, and sent them into small huddles to decide the criteria they would use for judging a good assignment title. I had two criteria in mind; to my great delight, they came up with my two, plus one of their own. Their criteria: that the assignment should involve them in finding facts and drawing conclusions; it should require them to go outside their normal working networks; and that it should have something to say about the social and economic issues facing the country.

I was moved to reflect that had I set a similar topic to a group of students in a business school in the UK, or the USA, they might have arrived at the first two criteria, but not the third. I wish I could show you those young faces, alight with a simple concern that what they had to do was make their country better.

October 1987 took me to New Zealand, to a conference of the New Zealand Association for Training and Development. There was the usual collection of talks and papers from people trying to push their expensive solutions and pet theories, but what stands out in my memory are the conversations I had with people who wanted to talk about the issues facing their country. In a way, that's not surprising, because New Zealand faces many serious problems and this is make-or-break time; but I carried away the memory of so many people, many of them young and not in positions of great authority, who not only spoke of the economic and social issues with wide-ranging knowledge, but also believed that their own contributions had the potential to make a difference.

March 1988 in Canberra, at the Australian Institute of Training and Development: the same thing. They had invited the Governor-General, and Professor Donald Horne, to talk to them about what kind of country they were and could become. I treasure the memory of Viv Read, one of the toughest and most creative people I know, speaking about some extraordinary industrial relations breakthroughs: the sub-text was 'We've got to get this right for the sake of the country'. And several others on the same lines; and again, that sense of young people believing that what they did in their everyday jobs could, and must, make a difference to their country.

There have been more experiences like that. Rias van Wyk, arguing passionately that the world was about to write off Africa as the 'gutter continent'. Albert Koopman, challenging his fellow managers to prepare for the time, ten years from now, when the average South African would be: male, eighteen years old, fatherless, just literate, and having engaged in at least one act of violence – and the managers picking up the challenge; the endless 'what does our country need next?' conversations in New Zealand, and the Aussie swashbuckling pride in achievement.

This is not a boast about how many stamps I have on my passport. I'm simply trying to draw a contrast between two parts of the English-speaking world that I know well, and to say that I feel deeply saddened that the average manager in the UK, or the USA, does not appear to feel the kind of larger commitment that I've seen, routinely, the other side of the Equator. Here (I write from the UK) the motivation seems to be for one's own career and jockeying for position within the organization; if you're lucky, a commitment to and pride in the organization; and there it ends. Maybe in this part of the world we've grown cynical and world-weary; maybe for my generation something died when they shot the man who said 'Ask not what your country can do for you; ask what you can do for your country'. And I'm not arguing for blind chauvinism. It's just that I can't help feeling that people who have a larger commitment are more likely to go the extra mile, more likely to show courage in dark places, and – well, to be just plain better people.

The same man – it was John F. Kennedy, of course – has the last word:

All this will not be finished in the first one hundred days. Nor will it be finished in the first one thousand days, nor in the life of this Administration, nor even perhaps in our lifetime on this planet.
But let us begin.

Appendix: How organizations grow and change

When I was a small child I conceived a desire to be a nuclear physicist when I grew up. I used to haunt the library in the miserable little town where I lived and take out every book I could find which seemed at all relevant to the subject. A popular author at that time was one George Gamow, who had a talent for pleasing diagrams, explanations, models, and metaphors. I devoured one of his books over the weekend and went for the next. Much to my disappointment, although the title was different, the text was virtually the same. Being a slow learner, I then swapped for another one of his and got a similar deal.

I don't want to do a Gamow on my readers; so I've put this chapter as an Appendix, because I'm describing a model that I've used in two previous books. It's a model that satisfies, for me, two criteria: a practical one and an epistemological one. (Allow me one long word: epistemology is the science of knowledge and explanations.) The practical criterion is that this is a model which almost anyone in an organization can identify with and find useful; given the emphasis in previous chapters on the need to share a map of organizational transformation, I find that this is the easiest map to share. The second criterion is that a first class theory predicts, a second class theory forbids, and a third class theory explains after the event; this model is a first class theory, and there aren't many of them around in the human sciences.

So, here in brief is an account of how organizations grow and change. If you've read it before, reflect please that for me also this is like being Elizabeth Taylor's eighth husband: I know what I have to do, but the problem is to make it interesting.

In the life-cycle of most organizations it is possible to see clear patterns of growth and transition. For example, many of them start small, and are characterized by a climate of innovativeness, high risk-taking, informality, closeness to the market, loose structure etc. In this, the *pioneering,* stage the influence of the founder(s) is very clearly felt, and the organization is the classic small business or entrepreneurial enterprise.

If the product or service is successful, and the organization continues to grow, then inevitably there will be a crisis. Any or all of the following can bring about the crisis: the size of the organization becomes too big for one manager to manage; the need for more specialist input; the need for finance; the retirement or death of the pioneer; the impact of competition (particularly when it learns from the pioneer's mistakes); the informal style leading to 'communication problems', etc. etc. The word crisis actually means change, and the crisis need not be fatal; in fact two of the three common trajectories of organizational failure are associated with mismanaging the pioneering crisis (see Figure A.1).

Trajectory 1   Trajectory 2

Figure A.1   Pioneering crisis trajectories

In the first trajectory the organization never becomes successful and disappears after a short while, and in the second trajectory the organization goes 'up like a rocket and down like a stick' through over-trading and related follies.

From observing organizations in the pioneering crisis an important lesson can be learned: in times of crisis people have a tendency to do more of what made them successful yesterday. And in the pioneering crisis, the last thing the organization needs is more of the 'pioneering' behaviour (e.g. frantic Laker commercials or new Sinclair inventions). To get out of trouble, the organization requires *systems and controls*; and thus, if it survives, it moves towards a climate in which formal systems are introduced to make things more predictable. Thus in the systems stage we see organizations with formal structures; divisions between line and staff, head office and divisions; rules and procedures; formalized planning; specialist functions; formal relations with unions, etc. The purpose of these influences is to make life more predictable, and in the early stages of their introduction people tend to sigh with relief as they now know where they stand and what is expected of them. (An important lesson to remember for those of us who feel that the systems are throttling us – once they were the medicine needed to lift the organization out of a moribund state.)

The systems stage, too, comes to outlive its usefulness. Sooner or later, the systems start to feel as if they are running the organization. There are grumbles about the length of time it takes to get decisions; a low-risk mentality; too much influence from head office, and/or specialists taking away line managers' discretion and decision making; distance from the customer; too much power in the hands of unions; a prevalence of bureaucracy; and a tendency to run life by the rule-book. If the response to this crisis is the same as that to the pioneering crisis, i.e. do more of what made the organization successful yesterday, then the rules will be tightened; procedures made more onerous; more committees, more dotted lines on the organization chart; more and more discretion taken away from line managers; the authority of head office increased; and the climate for risk-taking reduced even further. This is the systems crisis, and it too has its typical trajectory (see Figure A.2) in which the organization makes a serious mistake, fails to learn from

Trajectory 3

Figure A.2.   Systems crisis trajectory

it, and meets the next serious challenge with its resources depleted and its options foreshortened.

The systems crisis can be, and often is, made worse by a combination of the following factors:

1   It is more difficult to see than the pioneering crisis, because one of its characteristics is the remoteness of senior management from the shopfloor and the customer. The first stages are visible to the customer contact staff, their immediate managers, and of course the customers themselves. Senior management isolation, or its dependence on managing by figures rather than by insight, is likely to ensure that it only finds out about the crisis when a major customer leaves, the stock-market starts to sell the shares, or government introduces legislation to make them more customer-responsive.

2   The organization can often cushion itself against the crisis if it enjoys a monopoly or protected position within the national or local economy. Some are very good at playing the 'you wouldn't want 17 per cent unemployment just before a by-election, would you . . . so please can we have a hand-out' game.

3   The stabilizing managers, the people who are good at systems and controls, are often the least flexible in adopting new styles (see Chapter Six on corporate concrete for a fuller and, I hope, compassionate treatment thereof). If the organization recruited and rewarded too many such people in the early stages, without an eye to the later need for flexibility, then it finds it has an over-representation of those managers who are best, by nature, at solving problems by applying past experience, and less able to envision new solutions.

The way out of the systems crisis is one which a number of firms in the Western (and perhaps, with *glasnost*, the Soviet) economy are beginning to find. It means moving towards the *integrated* stage, which is characterized by the following climate:

1   Decentralization.
2   Delegation of authority (as opposed to work) to line managers.
3   A move from controlling systems towards enabling systems, and a concerted attempt to bust the bureaucracy.
4   A change in the role of head office and specialist functions, from being 'custodians of the word No' to a combined in-house consultancy and tame merchant bank.

5   A move towards a more entrepreneurial climate, with positive encouragement of risk taking and innovation.
6   A move towards getting back in touch with the customers and trying to understand and please them.
7   A move away from formal relationships with trade unions towards direct contact between managers and managed.
8   A re-emergence of the charismatic leader, and stress on personal leadership at all levels.

One very important point: there's nothing particularly good or bad about any particular stage. What is important is the appropriateness of the organizational structure for the stage it is at, and the ability of people within the organization to spot when yesterday's medicine has become tomorrow's poison. I'm fairly sure that each and every organization has to go through this process; though I also believe that an organization entering the systems stage today can, by learning from the example of their forebears, ensure that they do not experience the kind of concretization that happened to organizations now in the systems crisis. If you look at the history of some of the micro-technology organizations, many of which tried to be born into the integrated stage, you see that often they found themselves in a tangled mess and had to go back and install some order within the chaos. Properly managed, the journey through the three stages can be trouble-free; the problems come only when people assume that tomorrow will always be the same as yesterday, which allows me to indulge in a bit of fantasy. When I've been helping organizations to identify the key skills to manage their organization, I've often been told that it's not solely a manager's skills and experience which count – the high fliers also have the skill of timing. How I would love to analyse the make-up and acquisition of that skill! Somewhere, on an old knitting pattern, I wrote down ten key points. I may find it one day. But I know that one of the key points was the ability to know when what is needed is more of the same, and when what is needed is something different. And that ability, of course, is a necessary part of managing the process of organizational transformation, so that David doesn't wake up one day and find himself imprisoned in marble.

If by any chance you want to work out where your organization is, here's one of the diagnostic instruments I use to promote discussion:

Name: _____

Position: _____

ORGANIZATION DIAGNOSIS INSTRUMENT:

Instructions for completion:

This instrument is designed to allow you to diagnose the current state of development of your organization.

There are 10 questions per page. Place a tick in column 1 for each statement which, in your opinion, is broadly true of your organization. If you wish to differentiate your own department or division from the rest of the organization, use column 2 to describe it.

The questions are designed to prompt thought rather than to be necessary and sufficient indicators.

At the end, take a look at your pattern of answers, and in the light of the presentation on organization growth and change, make your decision about where your organization is.

Pioneering Stage

		1	2
1	The people who started our organization are still around and running it		
2	There has always been a high level of inventiveness in our organization		
3	The organization is growing fast, from a small base		
4	The organization has only one main office, plant, or factory		
5	The organization pays close attention to the needs of individual customers, and to personal service		
6	There have never been many laid down procedures, job descriptions, policy statements, etc.		
7	There has never been much paperwork, and people tend to communicate face-to-face		
8	The boss and the top team are technical experts, with a lot of 'hands-on' involvement with the technical details of the product or service		
9	There are few, if any, specialist staff departments		
10	The 'culture' feels high-risk, insecure, with the possibility of large rewards or major failures		
Total:			

Pioneering crisis

		1	2
1	The people who started our organization have recently retired or sold out		
2	Our organization has recently grown so much in size, or become so geographically dispersed, that it is difficult to know everyone		
3	People grumble about lack of proper planning, and a style of management by crisis		
4	Lack of proper record-keeping is starting to affect our efficiency		
5	Customers and/or employees are worried about equity and fairness of treatment		
6	In order to fund new investment, it is necessary to seek external financing		
7	Competitors have come into the market we recently created, and are gaining on us		
8	The top team feel that they are spending too much time on administration, and not enough on their technical expertise		
9	The top team are now managing managers rather than doing it themselves		
10	The informal communication system has broken down, and people grumble that they don't know what's going on		
Total:			

Systems stage

	1	2
1 There are policies and procedures written in manuals		
2 There is an organization chart		
3 There are formal systems such as job evaluation and performance appraisal for assessing employees' contribution		
4 There is a division into line and staff management, and perhaps into head office and divisions		
5 There are formal systems for scheduling work and forward planning		
6 There are formal systems for getting projects approved, gaining access to internal resources		
7 Some aspects of technical perfection are sacrificed in order to achieve economies of scale in production or selling		
8 The influence of larger organizations is sought, by taking managers or systems from them; or imposed by mergers and takeovers		
9 Formal means of communicating with staff are introduced, perhaps by the recognition of trade unions		
10 The 'culture' feels as if a welcome element of predictability has been introduced through the systems and controls		
Total:		

Unbalanced system stage

	1	2
1 Equipment is bought or designed without consulting the people who will have to work with it		
2 People find it difficult to control the pace of their work		
3 People find it difficult to discover how well they have been doing		
4 Tasks or equipment are assigned to employees in such a way that economies of scale, or of specialization, result in the employees feeling a lack of ownership of the finished product		
5 People are reluctant to cross departmental boundaries when planning their work		
6 People become specialized too early in their careers, resulting in over-supply in some departments and under-supply in others, or in unfulfilled potential because vital experience is missing		
7 Communication with employees, other than on routine work matters, takes place through the trade union only		
8 Junior and middle managers have no way of making their voices heard		
9 People are judged on how well they conform to the system, and not on how well they advance the organization's ultimate objectives		
10 (In continuous process organizations) The employees have more than one immediate supervisor, and supervisors manage a constantly shifting team		
Total:		

Systems crisis

	1	2
1 People grumble about the length of time it takes to get decisions made, and the number of people involved		
2 There is little tolerance of risk, and people feel they have to 'play safe'		
3 Specialists and/or head office departments tell line managers what they have to do		
4 Junior managers have very little authority to take risks or spend money		
5 Junior or middle managers leave to start their own businesses because they find the atmosphere stultifying		
6 The organization uses its size or position in the market-place to manipulate customers into taking what they are given		
7 Business is lost to smaller, nimbler, more customer-oriented competitors		
8 There are destructive rivalries between departments, often at the expense of service to the customer or advancement of the business as a whole		
9 Reorganization is used as a substitute for tackling performance problems		
10 The 'culture' feels slow, conservative, too oriented towards head office, too slow to react to outside information or pressures		
Total:		

Integrated stage

	1	2
1 Management systems are designed so as to reduce the power of the centre in holding information, resources, and consent		
2 Systems and procedures are judged by how well they enable people to do things, not how well they control them		
3 Head office changes its role into that of an internal consultant and/or tame merchant bank		
4 Authority is consciously devolved to more junior managers		
5 There is a genuine attempt to regain contact with the customers, find out what they want, and give it to them		
6 There are more or less conscious programmes to identify and develop in-house entrepreneurial skills		
7 Consultation and participation processes are used to raise ideas rather than just communicate management decisions		
8 There is renewed emphasis on charismatic leadership		
9 Senior managers manage the relationship between functions, not the functions themselves		
10 The 'culture' feels as if change is natural, and traditions have to be evaluated rather than automatically accepted		
Total:		

Now add up the scores for the different stages. Using these, and your knowledge of the organization, put a circle where you believe your organization (and, if you made the distinction, your own division or department) to be:

A MODEL OF ORGANIZATIONAL GROWTH AND CHANGE

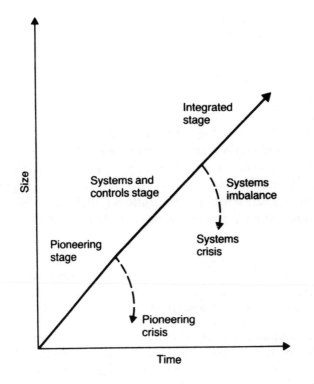

Sources and further reading

If this part of the book doesn't look as full as it might, or is not satisfactorily laden with scholarly references, I'm sorry. Much of my reading is chosen to promote knight's-move thinking rather than send me down a fixed track, and other readers might not agree with my selection of inspirational literature. However, the following books represent gems that I've quoted from, and wouldn't be without:

Charles Handy's *Understanding Organisations* (Penguin) is still the best single book about how organizations work. People I've recommended it to have telephoned me to thank me for it.

David Halberstam's *The Reckoning* is, like his earlier *The Best and the Brightest*, a stunning analysis of what happens when the low-risk bean counters come to rule an organization. Because Halberstam is not an organizational historian, and therefore doesn't use the language of organization theorists, his analysis is the more compelling. He's got it in for Robert MacNamara, first at Ford and then at the Department of Defence, showing how the spirit dies when you try to run an organization by the numbers. The former book is about the Vietnam War; in *The Reckoning* he turns his attention to the failure of the US car industry, and his account should be required reading for any manager, anywhere. It's that good. And Joseph Trento's *Prescription for Disaster*

(Harrap) shows the same insidious philosophy inside NASA – another dream killed by the bureaucrats.

If you want to follow up the hints that the Myers-Briggs Type Indicator is a useful instrument for encouraging people to talk about their strengths and how they can complement each other, *Please Understand Me* by David Kiersey and Marilyn Bates (Prometheus Nemesis Press) is a delightful, insightful book.

The best analysis of leadership in action I know comes from Norman Dixon, whose *On the Psychology of Military Incompetence* is now a classic. It speaks to managers as well as generals; my copy's falling apart.

I can't resist mentioning Ann Sperber's biography *Murrow: his Life and Times*. This is an instance of knight's move thinking for certain; Murrow wasn't a manager, didn't work in industry, and most people don't know who I'm talking about when I say that he's one of my all-time heroes. But if you want to be nourished by the story of a really great, courageous communicator, one who changed the face of the world by his words delivered under circumstances that tested his courage to the limit, this is the book. It must also rank as one of the greatest biographies of all time for the sustained quality of its writing.

Albert Koopman's book is written with co-authors Nasser and Nel: called *The Corporate Crusaders*, it isn't (I believe) available outside South Africa, so you'll have to persuade someone who doesn't mind being banned from the England cricket team to bring you a copy. It's worth it.

Acknowledgements

The nicest part of writing a book is the point where you can thank
your friends and colleagues – and no matter how modest they are,
they can't stop you. I'm enormously lucky in having a network of
friends who are all, in their own ways, lovely and unusual people
with commitment to enabling people to live to their full potential.
If ever I could get them all in one room, we'd change the world.

First mention must go to Midi Berry and William Keyser, of
Mosaic Management Consulting Ltd. Their professionalism and
values set me challenging standards; their friendship is a delight.
Midi's the only person I know who's made of equal quantities
of steel and flowers. Sister Ann O'Sullivan, of Emmaus House
in Bristol, is an unflagging enthusiast for enabling people to get
in touch with, and enjoy using, all their potential; Enid Davies,
who died in June 1988, worked with Ann. At Enid's memorial
celebration one person said: 'When Enid was around, you could
not be anybody but your real self.' Her empathy and talent for
fable and story-telling made me think of her as like a sweeper in a
curling game; running before the stone, influencing its speed and
direction, never once touching it because where she touched was
where the stone would be. George Lafferty and Peter Farrell,
of NFP Associates in Glasgow, are the finest pair of hands-on
developers of people's potential I know; Bill Laidlaw, Managing
Director of Mosaic, and his colleague Jim Oliver have taught me
the same lessons at a strategic level. Not that anybody passing

the door when any of those four are behind it would believe me, because there seems to be too much laughter going on.

I treasure the experience of working with those colleagues in South Africa who are putting their expertise into making the country better for everyone: Ed Dexter and Randall Falkenberg at Contact Training; John and Hannelore van Ryneveld; Wille Marais and the gang at Old Mutual; and those (too many to mention by name) for whom their management development has included the occasional spell in jail. For them, every day is a test of values and commitment the like of which the rest of us never see.

I'm privileged to know some transformational leaders: Chris Green, Director of Network SouthEast, is the one you could write the reference book on. Then there's Graham Ridler, of Rothmans; and Armour Mitchell, in New Zealand, who has one particular smile reserved for occasions of busting the bureaucracy and uses it often. Tribute, too to Pat MacInerny, who was Chief Executive of Telecom New Zealand; he's the only person I've ever seen who recognized that he was a Stage II leader but not for Stage III, and stepped gracefully and contentedly aside. A quiet example, like the man in the Potomac who gave up his place in the rescue helicopter that others might be saved, but one I won't forget.

Finally, on even more personal a note: my thanks to Mr. Ted Watson, the surgeon in New Zealand who saved my life; Glenn Eyes, who did so much for me in intensive care; Mr. Bill Southwood, in Bath, who sewed the holes back up; Pauline Davies, who coped with the chaos, and George Copeman at the Midland Bank, who listened when I needed him; and Tara and Maitreya from Shambhala in Glastonbury.

Valerie Stewart,
Keinton Mandeville, Somerset.
October 1989.

Index

PROJECT LEADERSHIP

How to lead any project effectively

~~~~~~~~~~~~~~~~

How to get the best out of
your project team

~~~~~~~~~~~~~~~~

Plus a powerful Action
Summary with questions aimed
at enhancing performance

*"If you want a book that will start you thinking about people,
relationships and teams...try 'Project Leadership'."*
Project Management Today

*"...a thought-provoking book, interesting for its conceptual clarity and
for the light it sheds on many of the problem areas affecting
projects, and enjoyable for its easy, direct style."*
The Training Officer

A Gower Paperback

RIGHT EVERY TIME

How to think quality

~~~~~~~~~~~~~~~~

How to understand quality

~~~~~~~~~~~~~~~~

How to apply Deming's Principles and avoid the pitfalls

"For all managers interested in quality, this is probably the most interesting and comprehensible book they will find."
Management Week

"As a sequel to the highly successful 'Right First Time' this offering is also a winner and should be obligatory reading for anyone who desires advancement in the search for excellence."
Management

"One of the earliest practical exponents of quality control sets out its general principles, illustrated with instructive case studies."
Director

A Gower Paperback